Arduino and SCILAB based Projects

Authored by:

Rajesh Singh and Anita Gehlot

Electronics & Communication Department Lovely Professional University, India

&

Bhupendra Singh

Schematics Microelectronics, Dehradun, Uttrakhand, India

Arduino and SCILAB basedProjects

Authors: Rajesh Singh, Anita Gehlot and Bhupendra Singh

ISBN (Online): 9789811410925

ISBN (Print): 9789811410918

First published in 2019.

need for a court order if at any point you breach any terms of this License Agreement. In no event will any delay or failure by Bentham Science Publishers in enforcing your compliance with this License Agreement constitute a waiver of any of its rights.

3. You acknowledge that you have read this License Agreement, and agree to be bound by its terms and conditions. To the extent that any other terms and conditions presented on any website of Bentham Science Publishers conflict with, or are inconsistent with, the terms and conditions set out in this License Agreement, you acknowledge that the terms and conditions set out in this License Agreement shall prevail.

Bentham Science Publishers Pte. Ltd.
80 Robinson Road #02-00
Singapore 068898
Singapore
Email: subscriptions@benthamscience.net

BENTHAM SCIENCE

CONTENTS

PREFACE i
   ACKNOWLEDGEMENTS i
   CONFLICT OF INTEREST i

SECTION A: ARDUINO AND ITS INTERFACING

CHAPTER 1 INTRODUCTION TO ARDUINO AND ARDUINO IDE AND
TOOLBOX_ARDUINO_V3 1
   1.1. ARDUINO UNO 2
   1.2. ARDUINO MEGA 3
   1.3. ARDUINO NANO 4
   1.4. INTRODUCTION TO ARDUINO I/O PACKAGE FOR SCILAB 6
      1.4.1. Steps to Upload Scilab Package in Arduino 6

CHAPTER 2 ARDUINO INTERFACING WITH SENSORS 7
   2.1. INTERFACING OF A CAPACITIVE TOUCH PROXIMITY SENSOR 7
      2.1.1. Capacitive Touch Proximity Sensor 8
         2.1.1.1. Circuit Diagram 9
         2.1.1.2. Program Code for Arduino Nano 10
   2.2. INTERFACING OF AN AC CURRENT SENSOR 11
      2.2.1. AC Current Sensor 12
         2.2.1.1. Circuit Diagram 13
         2.2.1.2. Program Code for Arduino Nano 15
   2.3. INTERFACING OF AC VOLTAGE SENSOR 16
      2.3.1. Circuit Diagram 18
      2.3.2. Program Code for Arduino Nano 19
   2.4. INTERFACING OF DC VOLTAGE SENSOR 21
      2.4.1. Circuit Diagram 22
      2.4.2. Program Code for Arduino Nano 23
   2.5. INTERFACING OF DC CURRENT SENSOR 24
      2.5.1. Circuit Diagram 26
      2.5.2. Program Code for Arduino Nano 27

CHAPTER 3 ARDUINO AND SERIAL COMMUNICATION 29
   3.1. SERIAL COMMUNICATION WITH 2.4 GHZ RF MODEM 29
      3.1.1. Circuit Diagram 32
         3.1.1.1. Circuit Diagram of Transmitter Section 32
         3.1.1.2. Circuit Diagram of Receiver Section 33
      3.1.2. Program Code 34
         3.1.2.1. Transmitter Program 34
         3.1.2.2. Receiver Program 36
   3.2. SERIAL COMMUNICATION WITH GSM MODEM 39
      3.2.1. Circuit Diagram 40
      3.2.2. Program Code 41

CHAPTER 4 INTRODUCTION TO SCILAB AND GUI WITHOUT TOOLBOX 44
   4.1. SCILAB GUI 44
      Steps to design GUI in Scilab 44

SECTION B: ARDUINO_1.1 PACKAGE WITH SCILAB

CHAPTER 5 SCILAB ARDUINO_1.1 PACKAGE (USING TOOLBOX_ ARDUINO_V3.INO) 48
   5.1. STEPS TO INSTALL PACKAGE IN ARDUINO 48
   5.2. BLOCKS OF SCILAB XCOS 50
      Building Blocks of XCOS 50
   5.3. DIGITAL READ 52
      5.3.1. Circuit Diagram 53
   5.4. DIGITAL WRITE 54
      5.4.1. Circuit Diagram 55
   5.5. DIGITAL READ AND WRITE 56
      5.5.1. Circuit Diagram 58
   5.6. ANALOG READ WITH POTENTIOMETER 58
      5.6.1. Circuit Diagram 61
   5.7. ANALOG READ WITH TEMPERATURE SENSOR 62
      5.7.1. Circuit Diagram 63
   5.8. ANALOG READ WRITE 64
      5.8.1. Circuit Diagram 66

CHAPTER 6 SERVO MOTOR CONTROL WITH ARDUINO_1.1 PACKAGE 69
   6.1. CIRCUIT DIAGRAM 70

CHAPTER 7 MOTION DETECTION SYSTEM WITH ARDUINO_1.1 PACKAGE 73
      Pir Motion Sensor 74
   7.1. CIRCUIT DIAGRAM 75

CHAPTER 8 TWO AXIS SOLAR TRACKER WITH ARDUINO_1.1 PACKAGE 78
      Servo Motor 79
   8.1. CIRCUIT DIAGRAM 79

CHAPTER 9 ENVIRONMENT PARAMETER MONITORING SYSTEM WITH ARDUINO_1.1 PACKAGE 82
      IR Sensor 83
      Gas Sensor 84
      The Proximity & Touch Sensor 84
      LM35 84
   9.1. CIRCUIT DIAGRAM 85

CHAPTER 10 ENVIRONMENT PARAMETER MONITORING ROBOT WITH ARDUINO_1.1 PACKAGE 88
   10.1. CIRCUIT DIAGRAM 89

CHAPTER 11 PID CONTROLLER FOR HEATER WITH ARDUINO_1.1 PACKAGE 92
   11.1. CIRCUIT DIAGRAM 94

SECTION C: SCILAB GUI WITHOUT ARDUINO_1.1 PACKAGE

CHAPTER 12 WIRELESS BUILDING AUTOMATION SYSTEM 96
   12.1. CIRCUIT DIAGRAM 98
      12.1.1. Connections of Transmitter Section 98
      12.1.2. Connections of Receiver Section 100
   12.2. PROGRAM CODE 101
      12.2.1. Program Code for Transmitter Section 101
      12.2.2. Program Code for Receiver Section 103

12.3. GRAPHICAL USER INTERFACE IN SCILAB 107

CHAPTER 13 WIRELESS ROBOT CONTROL WITH SCILAB GUI 111

   13.1. CIRCUIT DIAGRAM 113

      13.1.1. Connections For Transmitter Section. 113

      13.1.2. Connections For Receiver Section. 114

   13.2. PROGRAM CODE 116

      13.2.1. Program Code For Transmitter Section (Scilab Side) 116

      13.2.2. Program Code for Receiver Section. 118

   13.3. GRAPHICAL USER INTERFACE IN SCILAB 122

BIBLIOGRAPHY 125

SUBJECT INDEX 126

PREFACE

The primary objective of writing this book is to provide a platform for the beginners to get started with Arduino and its interfacing with SCILAB. The book provides the basic knowledge of the programming and interfacing of the devices with Arduino and SCILAB.

This book provides basics to advanced knowledge of Arduino and its interfacing with input/output devices (display devices, actuators, sensors), communication modules (RF modem, Zigbee) and SCILAB. This would be beneficial for the people who want to get started with embedded system projects. It provides embedded system based on Arduino with simulation, programming and interfacing with SCILAB, all at a single platform. Arduino interfacing with SCILAB with and without Arduino_1.1 packages are included. Basics of the Arduino are covered in section-A, section-B covers interfacing with Scilab Arduino_1.1 package and section-C covers projects without Scilab Arduino_1.1 package.

The concept which makes this book unique is descriptions of real time project prototypes with programming and simulation of Arduino and SCILAB. This book is entirely based on the practical experience of the authors, while undergoing projects with the students and industries. Although the circuits and programs mentioned in the text are tested, but in case of any mistake we extend our sincere apologies. Any suggestions to improve the contents of book are always welcome and will be appreciated and acknowledged.

ACKNOWLEDGEMENTS

We acknowledge the support from 'Nutty Engineer' to use its products to demonstrate and explain the working of the systems. We would like to thank 'BENTHAM SCIENCE' for encouraging our idea about this book and the support to manage the project efficiently.

We are grateful to the honorable Chancellor (Lovely Professional University) Ashok Mittal, Mrs. Rashmi Mittal (Pro Chancellor, LPU), Dr. Ramesh Kanwar (Vice Chancellor, LPU), Dr. Loviraj Gupta (Executive Dean, LPU) for their support. In addition, we are thankful to our family, friends, relatives, colleagues and students for their moral support and blessings.

CONFLICT OF INTEREST

The author(s) declared no conflict of interest regarding the contents of each of the chapters of this book.

Rajesh Singh and Anita Gehlot
Electronics & Communication Dept.
Lovely Professional University,
India

Bhupendra Singh
Schematics Microelectronics,
Dehradun,
India

CHAPTER 1

Introduction to Arduino and Arduino IDE and toolbox_arduino_v3

Abstract: Arduino is an open source platform and easy to use. The chapter discusses the brief description to board. Steps to download and upload Scilab XCOS files to Arduino are also discussed, to get started with it. Arduino is an open-source electronic prototyping platform based on flexible, easy-to-use hardware and software. It is intended for persons interested in creating interactive objects or environments.

Arduino can sense the environment by receiving input from sensors and can affect its surroundings by controlling devices. Microcontroller on the board is programmed using Arduino programming language and the Arduino development environment. Arduino projects can be stand-alone or they can communicate with software running on a computer.

Keywords: Arduino, Arduino IDE, Open Source Platform.

Arduino is a user friendly open-source platform. Arduino has on board microcontroller and IDE is used to program it. As compared to similar platforms it is easy to program and has many advantages over them.

Advantages:

Low Cost - Arduino boards are of relatively low-cost as compared to other microcontroller platforms.

Cross-platform - The Arduino Software (IDE) is compatible with Windows, Macintosh OSX, and Linux operating systems, which most of microcontroller systems are not.

User Friendly - The Arduino Software (IDE) is user friendly and easy-to-use for beginners and much flexibility for skilled programmers.

Open source - The Arduino is an open source software and can be programmed with C, C++ or AVR-C languages.

Rajesh Singh, Anita Gehlot & Bhupendra Singh

Arduino platform comprises of a microcontroller. It can be connected to PC *via* a USB cable. It is freely accessible and can be easily downloaded from http://www.arduino.org/downloads. It can also be modified by the programmer. In the market different versions of Arduino boards are available and depending on the requirement of user.

1.1. ARDUINO UNO

The Arduino/Genuino Uno has on board ATmega328 microcontroller. It has six analog input ports (A0-A5). Each pin can operate on 0-5V of voltage. It has 14 digital I/O pins out of which 6 are PWM output, 2 KB SRAM, 1 KB EEPROM and operates at 16 MHz of frequency.

The pins details are as follows-

Input and Output-Arduino unohave 14 digital pins can be used as an input or output. These pins operate at 5 volts and individual provide or receive 40mA current. It has an internal pull-up resistor of 20-50 kohms. The Arduino Uno has six analog inputs named as A0 through A5. The resolution of ADC is 10bits (means 1024 digital levels). In addition, there are some pins have specialized functions, as follows-

Serial: The Arduino uno has pins 0 (RX) for receive transistor-transistor-logic (TTL) data and 1 (TX) for transmit transistor-transistor-logic (TTL) data using UART mode.

External Interrupts: The pins 2 and 3 are used as interrupt pins and can be used to read a rising or falling edge, or a change in value.

PWM: The pins 3, 5, 6, 9, 10, and 11 of Arduino uno are used as 'Pulse Width Modulation'.

SPI: The 10 (SS), 11 (MOSI), 12 (MISO), 13 (SCK) of Arduino uno is used as serial peripheral interface (SPI).

LED: pin 13 of Arduino uno board have inbuilt LED.

TWI: The pins A4 or SDA pin and A5 or SCL in Arduino uno used as two wire interface (TWI) or inter IC communication (I2C).

AREF: Aref pin of Arduino uno board provide reference voltage for the analog inputs.

Reset: The reset pin is used to reset the microcontroller.

Fig.(**1.1**) shows the Arduino Uno board.

Fig. (1.1). View of Arduino Uno.

1.2. ARDUINO MEGA

The Arduino Mega has on board ATmega2560 microcontroller. It has on board 16 analog inputs, 54 digital I/O, USB connection, 4 UART, power jack and reset button. It operates on 16 MHz frequency. The board can be operated with 5-12 volts of external power, if supplied more than this it can damage the board. It has on board 256 KB flash memory, 8 KB SRAM, 4 KB EEPROM. Table **1.1** shows the pin description of Arduino Mega.

Table 1.1. Pin Description of Arduino Mega.

Pin	Description
Vin	The external voltage to the Arduino board.
+5V	Output a regulated 5V
3.3 V	On board 3.3 volt supply
GND	Ground
IOREF	Provides the voltage reference and select appropriate power source
Serial0	Transmits and receives serial data, Pins: 0(Rx) 1(Tx)
Serial1	Transmits and receives serial data, Pins: 19(Rx) 18(Tx)
Serial2	Transmits and receives serial data, Pins: 17(Rx) 16(Tx)
External Interrupts	Trigger an interrupt on low value (Pins 2 (interrupt 0), 3(interrupt1), 18 (interrupt5), 19(interrupt 4), 20 (interrupt2))

Pin	Description
PWM	Provides 8 bit PWM output (pins: 2 to 13 and 44 to 46)
SPI	Supports SPI communication (Pins: 53(SS), 51(MOSI), 50 (MISO) and 52 (SCK))
LED	LED driven by pin 13
TWI	Supports TWI communication (Pins: 20 (SDA), 21(SCL))
AREF	Reference voltage for the analog inputs
Reset	It is used to reset the onboard microcontroller

Fig. (**1.2**) shows the Arduino Mega board.

Fig.(1.2). Arduino Mega Board.

1.3. ARDUINO NANO

Arduino Nano is based on ATmega328 and is a small, complete, and breadboard-friendly board (Arduino Nano 3.x). It has same functionality of the Arduino uno, but with a different package. It lacks a DC power jack and works with a Mini-B USB cable instead of a standard one.

Arduino Software (IDE) is used to program it. Fig. (**1.3**) shows the snapshot for Arduino Nano.

Fig. (1.3). Arduino Nano.

Arduino Nano is a smallest, user friendly board and can easily be mounted on a breadboard. Nano automatically senses and switches to the higher potential source of power, which eliminates the need of the power select jumper. The new version 3.0 comes with ATMEGA328 which offers more programming and data memory space.

Specifications of Arduino Nano are as follows:

Microcontroller	Atmel ATmega328
Operating Voltage (logic level)	5 V
Input Voltage (recommended)	7-12 V
Input Voltage (limits)	6-20 V
Digital I/O Pins	14 (of which 6 provides PWM output)
Analog Input Pins	8
DC Current per I/O Pin	40 mA
Flash Memory	32 KB (of which 2KB used by bootloader)
SRAM	2 KB
EEPROM	1 KB
Clock Speed	16 MHz
Dimensions	0.70" x 1.70"

1.4. INTRODUCTION TO ARDUINO I/O PACKAGE FOR SCILAB

Arduino can be programed with different IOs including digital IO, analog IO, encoder input, PWM output, *etc.* Data flow can be controlled, using the provided IOs. Scilab/Xcos can acquire the data, process the data, and send the control signal back to the board. Fig. (**1.4**) shows Arduino interaction with Scilab.

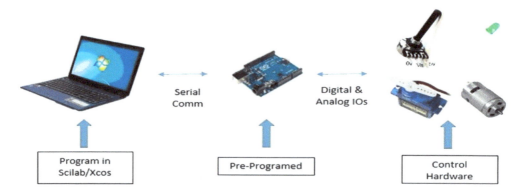

Fig. (1.4). Arduino interaction with Scilab.

Scilab is an open source, user friendly, state-of-the-art cross-platform numerical computational package and a high-level, numerically oriented programming language. It can be used for signal and image processing, statistical analysis, internet of things, data mining, *etc.*

Scilab-Arduino interface is devoted to the control of Arduino from Scilab. The interface helps the user to perform embedded systems experiments on Arduino board using Scilab code and through GUI based simulation environment (XCOS).

1.4.1. Steps to Upload Scilab Package in Arduino

1. Download the Scilab setup from http://www.scilab.org
2. Download the Arduino toolbox for Scilab from http://atoms.scilab.org/toolboxes/arduino
3. Download Arduino IDE software to write code for Arduino Nano from http://arduino.cc/en/Main/Software

Download the program file from toolbox_arduino_v3.ino and open in Arduino IDE and upload it into Arduino Nano Board.

CHAPTER 2

Arduino Interfacing with Sensors

Abstract: This chapter describes the interfacing of analog and digital sensors with an Arduino board. The sensor is a device which detects the change in physical, electrical or other parameters and generates an electrical or optical signal as output. The sensor which produces a continuous output signal is known as an analog sensor and the sensor which changes the output status on occurrence of an event is called the digital sensor. The voltage of an output signal of an analog sensor is proportional to the quantity measured. The examples of the digital sensor include capacitive touch proximity sensor, and fire sensor and the analog sensors are voltage sensor, and current sensor.

Keywords: Arduino, Analog Sensor, Digital Sensor.

2.1. INTERFACING OF A CAPACITIVE TOUCH PROXIMITY SENSOR

The objective is to describe the interfacing of a capacitive touch proximity sensor with an Arduino Nano. A system is designed to display the status of a capacitive touch proximity sensor (digital sensor) on a liquid crystal display and to correspondingly change the status of a LED 'ON/OFF'. The system comprises an Arduino Nano, a DC 12V/1Amp adaptor, a 12V to 5V converter, a 3.3V converter, a capacitive touch proximity sensor, a liquid crystal display, a resistor 330 ohm, and a LED. Fig. (**2.1**) shows the block diagram of the system.

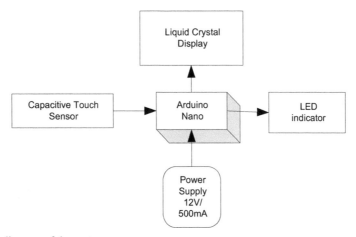

Fig. (2.1). Block diagram of the system.

Rajesh Singh, Anita Gehlot & Bhupendra Singh

Table **2.1** describes the component list, required to develop the system.

Table 2.1. Component list.

Component	Quality
Power Supply 12V/500mA	1
+12V to 5V converter	1
Power supply patch/ breakout	1
Arduino Nano	1
Capacitive touch sensor	1
LED	1
330 ohm resistor	1
LCD16*2	1
LCD patch/ breakout board for 16*2	1
M-F connector jumper wire	20
F-F connector jumper wire	20
M-M connector jumper wire	20

Note: All components are available at www.nuttyengineer.com

2.1.1. Capacitive Touch Proximity Sensor

The capacitive touch proximity sensor is capable of detecting the touch. It is simple to use and is automatically calibrated. It has on board IC TTP223. The output of the sensor can be configured as active 'HIGH' or active 'LOW' logic. The sensor is compatible with the microcontroller without any intermediate circuit. Fig. (**2.2**) shows the capacitive touch proximity sensor.

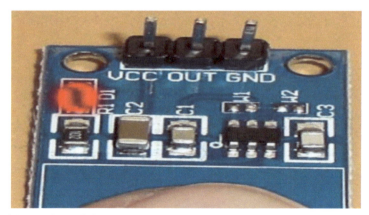

Fig. (2.2). Capacitive touch proximity sensor.

2.1.1.1. Circuit Diagram

The connections for the circuit are as follows-

1. +12V and GND (ground) terminals of the power adaptor are connected with the female DC jack of the Arduino Nano.
2. +5V and GND (ground) terminals of the power supply are connected to +5V and GND pins of the LCD, respectively.
3. RS, RW and E control pins of the LCD are connected to D12, GND, and D11 pins of the Arduino Nano respectively.
4. D4, D5, D6, D7 pins of the LCD patch are connected to D10,. D9, D8, and D7 pins of the Arduino Nano respectively.
5. Anode terminal of the LED is connected to D5 pin of the Arduino through a 330 ohm resistor and cathode terminal to the GND (Ground).
6. +Vcc, GND, and OUT pins of the sensor are connected to +5V, GND, and D6 pins of the Arduino Nano respectively.

Fig. (**2.3**) shows the circuit diagram for the interfacing of the capacitive touch proximity sensor with the Arduino.

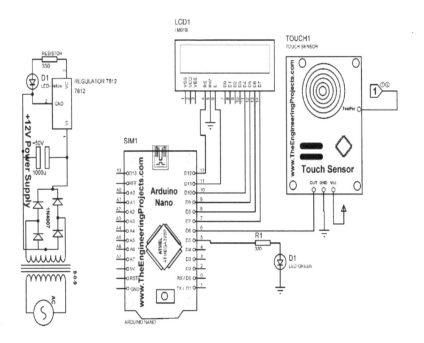

Fig. (2.3). Circuit diagram for the interfacing of capacitive touch proximity sensor with Arduino.

2.1.1.2. Program Code for Arduino Nano

```
#include <LiquidCrystal.h> // add Library of LCD

LiquidCrystallcd(12, 11, 10, 9, 8, 7); // pins of LCD are connected to Arduino Nano board

//////// LED and Sensor Pins

const int Touch_Sensor_Pin = 6; // connect touch sensor to pin7 of Arduino Nano

const int LED_pin= 5; // connect LED to pin5 of Arduino Nano

int Touch_sensor_logic = 0; // assume integer

void setup()

{

lcd.begin(16, 2);// Initialise LCD 16*2

pinMode(LED_pin, OUTPUT);// set pin 5 as output

pinMode(Touch_Sensor_Pin, INPUT_PULLUP);// set pin 6 as input when sensor is in active LOW

lcd.setCursor(0,0); // set cursor of LCD

lcd.print("Touch sensor");// print string on LCD

lcd.setCursor(0,1); // set cursor of LCD

lcd.print("based system"); // print string on LCD

delay(2000); // set delay 0f 2000 mSec

}

void loop()

{

Touch_sensor_logic= digitalRead(Touch_Sensor_Pin); // read sensor

   if (Touch_sensor_logic == LOW) // check state

   {
```

```
lcd.clear(); // clear the LCD

lcd.setCursor(0,1); // set cursor of LCD

lcd.print("Touch Detected"); // print string on LCD

digitalWrite(LED_pin, HIGH); // make LED pin HIGH

delay(20); // wait for 20mSec

    }

    else

    {

lcd.clear(); // clear the LCD

lcd.setCursor(0,1); // set cursor of LCD

lcd.print("No Touch"); // print string on LCD

digitalWrite(LED_pin, LOW); // make LED pin HIGH

delay(20); // wait for 20mSec

    }

}
```

2.2. INTERFACING OF AN AC CURRENT SENSOR

The objective is to describe the interfacing of an AC current sensor with an Arduino Nano. A system is designed to display the status of an AC current sensor (analog sensor) on a liquid crystal display and to change the status of a LED 'ON/OFF' by setting a threshold level. The system comprises an Arduino Nano, a DC 12V/1Amp adaptor, a 12V to 5V, a 3.3V converter, an AC current sensor, a liquid crystal display, a resistor 330 ohm, and a LED. Fig. (**2.4**) shows the block diagram of the system.

Table **2.2** describes the components list required to develop the system.

Table 2.2. Component list.

Component	Quality
Power Supply 12V/500mA	1

(Table 2.2) cont.....

Component	Quality
+12V to 5V converter	1
Power supply patch/ breakout	1
Arduino Nano	1
AC current sensor	1
LED	1
330 ohm resistor	1
LCD16*2	1
LCD patch/ breakout board for 16*2	1
M-F connector jumper wire	20
F-F connector jumper wire	20
M-M connector jumper wire	20

Note: All components are available at www.nuttyengineer.com

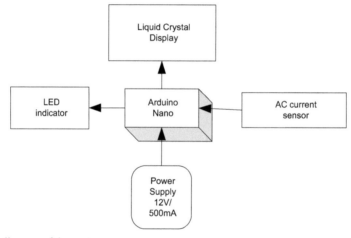

Fig. (2.4). Block diagram of the system.

2.2.1. AC Current Sensor

The current transformer (CT) acts as sensor, which can measure the alternating current in the electrical circuits. The sensor is capable of handling 0-100A current at input and generates 0-50mA at the output. The applications of sensor include protection of AC motor, design of energy meter, air compressor and lightening equipment *etc.* Fig. (**2.5**) shows the non-invasive AC current sensor.

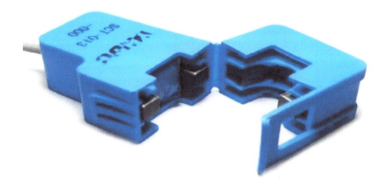

Fig. (2.5). Non invasive AC Current Sensor.

To interface an Arduino with an AC sensor, a signal conditioning circuit is required, so that it can meet the minimum acceptable input range (a positive voltage between 0V and an ADC reference voltage) for an analog input of the Arduino. The signal conditioning circuit can be designed with a biasing voltage divider (R1 & R2). Fig. (**2.6**) shows the signal conditional circuit for non-invasive AC current sensor.

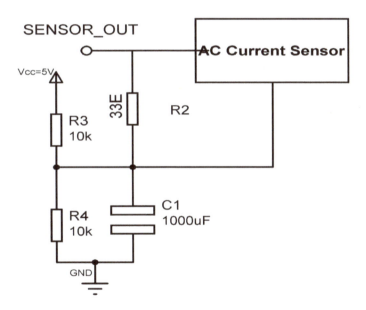

Fig. (2.6). Signal conditioning circuit for non invasive AC current sensor

2.2.1.1. Circuit Diagram

The connections for the circuit are as follows-

1. +12V and GND (ground) terminals of the power adaptor are connected to the female DC jack of the Arduino Nano.
2. +5V and GND (ground) pin of the power supply are connected to +5V and GND pins of the LCD respectively.
3. RS, RW and E control pins of the LCD are connected to D12, GND, D11 pins of the Arduino Nano respectively.
4. D4, D5, D6, D7 pins of the LCD are connected to D10. D9, D8, D7 pins of the Arduino Nano respectively.
5. Anode terminal of the LED is connected to D5 pin of the Arduino through a 330 ohm resistor and cathode terminal to the GND (Ground).
6. +Vcc, GND, OUT pins of sensor are connected to +5V, GND, A0 pins of the Arduino Nano respectively.

Fig. (**2.7**) shows the circuit diagram for the interfacing of AC current sensor with Arduino Nano.

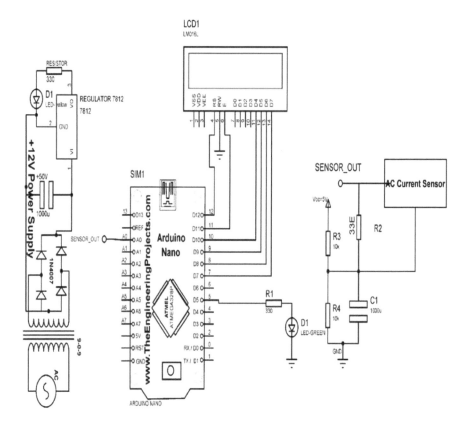

Fig. (2.7). Circuit diagram for the interfacing of AC current sensor with Arduino Nano.

2.2.1.2. Program Code for Arduino Nano

```
#include <LiquidCrystal.h> // add library of LCD

LiquidCrystallcd(12, 11, 10, 9, 8, 7); // connect pin of LCD to Arduino Nano

#include "EmonLib.h" // Include Emon Library

EnergyMonitor emon1; // Create an instance

double AC_CURRENT-Irms; // assume

sensor_status_indicator=5; // connect LED to pin5

void setup()

{

lcd.begin(16, 2);// Initialise LCD 16*2

emon1.current(1, 111.1); // Current: input pin, calibration.

lcd.setCursor(0,0); // set cursor on LCD

lcd.print("AC current"); // print string on LCD

lcd.setCursor(0,1); // // set cursor on LCD

lcd.print("Measurement"); // print string on LCD

delay(2000); // wait for 2000 mSec

}

void loop()

{

AC_CURRENT-Irms = emon1.calcIrms(1480); // Calculate Irms only

digitalWrite(sensor_status_indicator,HIGH); // Make indicator pin HIGH

lcd.clear(); // clear the contents of LCD

lcd.setCursor(0,0); // set cursor on LCD

lcd.print("AC current(Irms):"); // print string on LCD
```

lcd.setCursor(0,1); // set cursor on LCD

lcd.print(AC_CURRENT-Irms);

deley(30); // wait for 30 mSec

digitalWrite(sensor_status_indicator,LOW); // Make indicator pin LOW

delay(300); // wait for 300 mSec

}

2.3. INTERFACING OF AC VOLTAGE SENSOR

The objective is to describe the interfacing of AC voltage sensor with an Arduino Nano. A system is designed to display the status of AC voltage sensor (analog sensor) on liquid crystal display and change the status of a LED 'ON/OFF' by setting a threshold level. The system comprises of an Arduino Nano, a DC 12V/1Amp adaptor, a 12V to 5V, a 3.3V converter, an AC voltage sensor, a liquid crystal display, a resistor 330 ohm, and a LED. Fig. (**2.8**) shows the block diagram of the system.

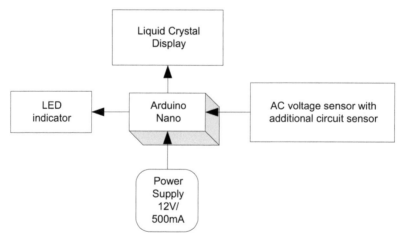

Fig. (2.8). Block diagram of the system.

Table **2.3** describes the component list, required to develop the system.

Table 2.3. Component list

Component	Quality
Power Supply 12V/500mA	1

(Table 2.3) cont.....

Component	Quality
+12V to 5V converter	1
Power supply patch/ breakout	1
Arduino Nano	1
AC voltage sensor	1
LED	1
330 ohm resistor	1
LCD16*2	1
LCD patch/ breakout board for 16*2	1
M-F connector jumper wire	20
F-F connector jumper wire	20
M-M connector jumper wire	20

Note: All components are available at www.nuttyengineer.com

Fig. (2.9). 9V AC Adaptor.

Fig. (**2.9**) shows a 9V AC adaptor. A 9V (rms) power adapter has positive voltage peak at 12.7V, and the negative peak at -12.7V. To convert the output of the adaptor to a waveform with a positive peak less than +5V and a negative peak more than 0V, a signal conditioning circuit is required. Fig. (**2.10**) shows a signal conditioning circuit. Two resistors R1 and R2 are connected to form a voltage divider, to scale down the power adaptor AC voltage. The resistors R3 and R4 are connected to provide the voltage bias. A capacitor C1(1µF to 10µF) provides a low impedance path to ground the AC signal. The values of R1 and R2 need to be chosen in such a way so that the combination can provide a peak voltage output of ~1V. For an AC-AC adapter with a 9V 'RMS' output, a resistor combination of 10k for R1 and 100k for R2 would be suitable:

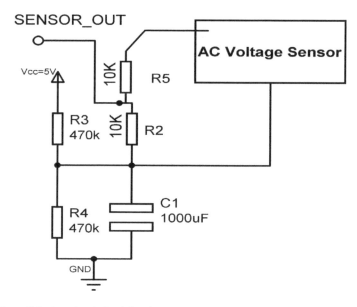

Fig. (2.10). Signal conditioning circuit for AC voltage sensor.

2.3.1. Circuit Diagram

The connections for the circuit are as follows-

1. +12V and GND (ground) terminals of the power adaptor are connected with female DC jack of the Arduino Nano.
2. +5V and GND (ground) pins of the power supply are connected to +5V and GND pins of the LCD respectively.
3. RS, RW and E control pins of the LCD are connected to D12, GND, D11 pins of the Arduino Nano respectively.
4. D4, D5, D6, D7 pins of the LCD are connected to D10. D9, D8, D7 pins of the Arduino Nano respectively.
5. Anode terminal of a LED is connected to D5 pin of the Arduino through a 330 ohm resistor and cathode terminal to the GND (Ground).
6. +Vcc, GND, OUT pins of the sensor are connected to +5V, GND, A0 pins of the Arduino Nano respectively.

Fig. (**2.11**) shows the circuit diagram for the interfacing of AC voltage sensor to Arduino Nano.

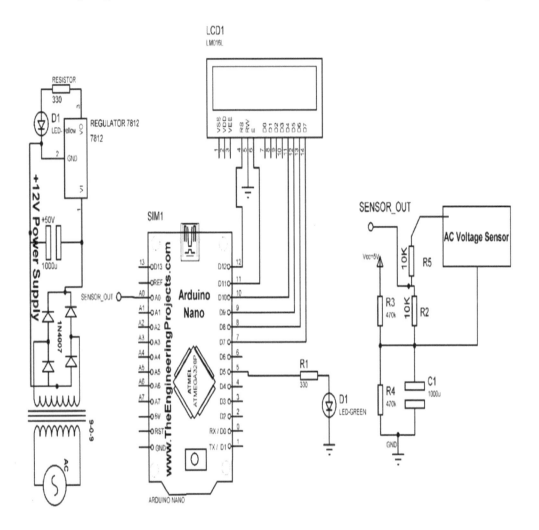

Fig. (2.11). Circuit diagram for the interfacing of AC voltage sensor to Arduino Nano.

2.3.2. Program Code for Arduino Nano

#include <LiquidCrystal.h> // add library of LCD

LiquidCrystallcd(12, 11, 10, 9, 8, 7); // LCD pin connected to Arduino Nano

#include "EmonLib.h"   // Include Emon Library

EnergyMonitor emon1;   // Create an instance

double AC_CURRENT-Irms; // assume double

```
sensor_status_indicator=5; // connect indicator to pinD5
void setup()
{
lcd.begin(16, 2);// Initialise LCD 16*2
emon1.voltage(2, 234.26, 1.7); // Voltage: input pin, calibration, phase_shift
lcd.setCursor(0,0); // set cursor on LCD
lcd.print("AC Voltage"); // print string on LCD
lcd.setCursor(0,1); // set cursor on LCD
lcd.print("Measurement"); // print string on LCD
delay(2000); // wait for 2000 mSec
}
void loop()

{
float supply_Voltage_from_input = emon1.Vrms; //extract Vrms into Variable
digitalWrite(sensor_status_indicator,HIGH); // make indicator pin HIGH
lcd.clear(); // clear LCD
lcd.setCursor(0,0); // set cursor on LCD
lcd.print("AC voltage(Vrms):"); // print value of rms voltage
lcd.setCursor(0,1); // set cursor on LCD
lcd.print(supply_Voltage_from_input);
deley(30); // wait for 30 mSec
digitalWrite(sensor_status_indicator,LOW); // make indicator pin LOW
delay(300); // wait for 300 mSec
```

2.4. INTERFACING OF DC VOLTAGE SENSOR

The objective is to describe the interfacing of DC voltage sensor with an Arduino Nano. A system is designed to display the status of DC voltage sensor (analog sensor) on liquid crystal display and change the status of a LED 'ON/OFF' by setting a threshold level. The system comprises of an Arduino Nano, a DC 12V/1Amp adaptor, a 12V to 5V, a 3.3V converter, a DC voltage sensor, a liquid crystal display, a resistor 330 ohm, and a LED. Fig. (**2.12**) shows the block diagram of the system. Fig. (**2.13**) shows the DC voltage sensor.

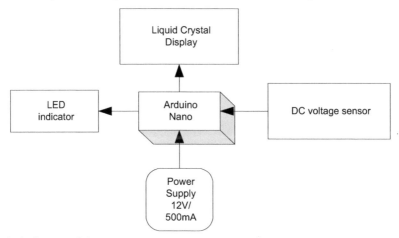

Fig. (2.12). Block diagram of the system.

Table **2.4** describes the component list, required to develop the system.

Table 2.4. Component list.

Components	Quality
Power Supply 12V/500mA	1
+12V to 5V converter	1
Power supply patch/ breakout	1
Arduino Nano	1
DC voltage sensor	1
LED	1
330 ohm resistor	1
LCD16*2	1
LCD patch/ breakout board for 16*2	1
M-F connector jumper wire	20

(Table 2.4) cont.....

Components	Quality
F-F connector jumper wire	20
M-M connector jumper wire	20

Note: All components are available at www.nuttyengineer.com

Fig. (2.13). DC voltage sensor.

2.4.1. Circuit Diagram

The connections of the circuit are as follows-

1. +12V and GND (ground) terminals of power adaptor are connected to female DC jack of the Arduino Nano.
2. +5V and GND (ground) pins of the power supply are connected to +5V and GND pins of the LCD respectively.
3. RS, RW and E pins of the LCD are connected to D12, GND, D11 pins of the Arduino Nano respectively.
4. D4, D5, D6, D7 pins of the LCD are connected to D10. D9, D8, D7 pins of the Arduino Nano respectively.
5. Anode terminal of a LED is connected to D5 pin of the Arduino through a 330 ohm resistor and cathode terminal to GND (Ground).
6. +Vcc, GND, OUT pins of the sensor are connected to +5V, GND, A0 pins of Arduino Nano respectively.

Fig. (**2.14**) shows circuit diagram for the interfacing of DC voltage sensor to Arduino Nano.

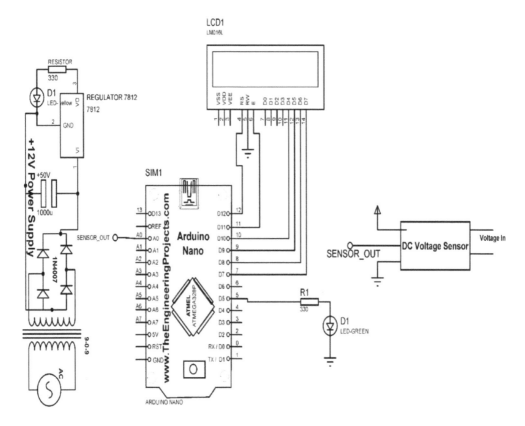

Fig. (2.14). Circuit diagram for the interfacing of DC voltage sensor to Arduino Nano.

2.4.2. Program Code for Arduino Nano

#include <LiquidCrystal.h> // add LCD library

LiquidCrystallcd(12, 11, 10, 9, 8, 7); // pins of LCD connect to Arduino Nano

int DC_Volatge_sensor_level=A0; // connect DC voltage sensor to pin A0

float DC_supply_Voltage_from_input=0; // assume float

void setup()

{

lcd.begin(16, 2);// Initialise LCD 16*2

lcd.setCursor(0,0); // set cursor on LCD

```
lcd.print("DC Voltage"); // print string on LCD

lcd.setCursor(0,1); // set cursor on LCD

lcd.print("Measurement"); // print string on LCD

delay(2000); // wait for 2 sec

}

void loop()

{

DC_Volatge_sensor_level = analogRead(A0);

DC_supply_Voltage_from_input = DC_Volatge_sensor_level * (5.0 / 1024.0) *
10;

lcd.clear(); // clear LCD

lcd.setCursor(0,0); // set cursor on LCD

lcd.print("DC voltage(Vdc):"); // print value on LCD with string

lcd.setCursor(0,1);

lcd.print(DC_supply_Voltage_from_input); // print value on LCD

delay(300); // wait for 300 mSec

}
```

2.5. INTERFACING OF DC CURRENT SENSOR

This section describes the interfacing of DC current sensor with an Arduino Nano. A system is designed to display the status of DC current sensor (analog sensor) on liquid crystal display and change the status of a LED 'ON/OFF' by setting a threshold level. The system comprises of an Arduino Nano, a DC 12V/1Amp adaptor, a 12V to 5V, a 3.3V converter, a DC current sensor, a liquid crystal display, a resistor 330 ohm, and a LED. Fig. (**2.15**) shows the block diagram of the system.

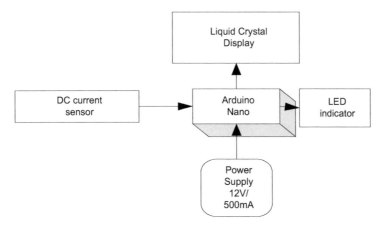

Fig. (2.15). Block diagram of the system.

Table **2.5** describes the component list, required to develop the system.

Table 2.5. Component list

Component	Quality
Power Supply 12V/500mA	1
+12V to 5V converter	1
Power supply patch/ breakout	1
Arduino Nano	1
DC current sensor	1
LED	1
330 ohm resistor	1
LCD16*2	1
LCD patch/ breakout board for 16*2	1
M-F connector jumper wire	20
F-F connector jumper wire	20
M-M connector jumper wire	20

Note: All components are available at www.nuttyengineer.com

Fig. (**2.16**) shows a DC current sensor. The current measurement range of the sensor is 20mA to 20A and sensitivity is 100mV/A.

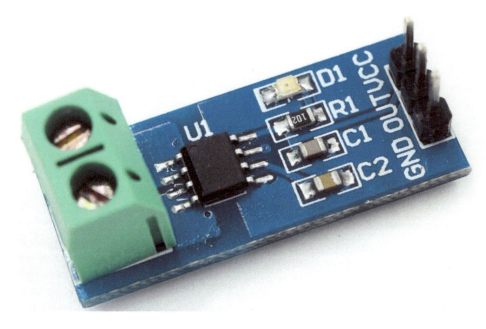

Fig. (2.16). DC current sensor.

2.5.1. Circuit Diagram

The connections of the circuit are as follows-

1. +12V and GND (ground) pins of power adaptor are connected to female DC jack of the Arduino Nano.
2. +5V and GND (ground) pins of the power supply are connected to +5V and GND pin of the LCD respectively.
3. RS, RW and E pins of the LCD are connected to D12, GND, D11 pins of the Arduino Nano board respectively.
4. D4, D5, D6, D7 pins of the LCD are connected to D10. D9, D8, D7 pins of the Arduino Nano respectively.
5. Anode terminal of a LED is connected to D5 pin of the Arduino through a 330 ohm resistor and cathode terminal to GND (Ground).
6. +Vcc, GND, OUT pins of the sensor are connected to +5V, GND, A0 pins of the Arduino Nano respectively.

Fig. (**2.17**) shows circuit digarm for the interfacing of DC current sensor with Arduino Nano.

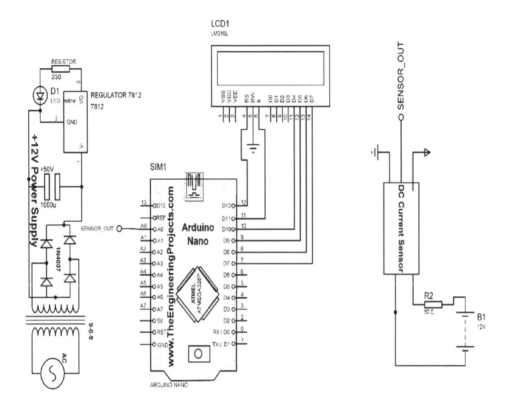

Fig. (2.17). Circuit digarm for the interfacing of DC current sensor with Arduino Nano.

2.5.2. Program Code for Arduino Nano

#include <LiquidCrystal.h> // add library of LCD

LiquidCrystallcd(12, 11, 10, 9, 8, 7); // pins of LCD connect to Arduino Nano

const int Current_sensor_pin = A0; // connect current sensor to A0 pin

int I_mVperAmp = 185; // use 100 for 20A Module and 66 for 30A Module

int Current_sensor_level= 0; // define integer

int I_ACSoffset = 2500; // take 2.5V as offset

double total_Voltage = 0; // define double

double Idc = 0; // assume double

```
void setup()
{
lcd.begin(16, 2);// Initialise LCD 16*2
lcd.setCursor(0,0); // set cursor on LCD
lcd.print("DC Current"); // print string on LCD
lcd.setCursor(0,1); // set cursor on LCD
lcd.print("Measurement"); //print string on LCD
delay(2000); // wait for delay 2000 mSec
}
void loop()
{
Current_sensor_level = analogRead(Current_sensor_pin); // read current sensor
total_Voltage = (RawValue / 1024.0) * 5000; // Gets you mV
Idc = ((total_Voltage - I_ACSoffset) / I_mVperAmp); // gets Idc
lcd.clear(); // clear previous contents of LCD
lcd.setCursor(0,0); // set cursor on LCD
lcd.print("DC voltage(Vdc):"); // print string on LCD
lcd.setCursor(0,1); // set cursor on LCD
lcd.print(Idc); // print the value of current on LCD
delay(300); // wait for 300 mSec
}
```

CHAPTER 3

Arduino and Serial Communication

Abstract: This chapter describes the serial communication supports device in microcontroller. Serial communication is the process of sending data bit wise on a communication channel, with a data rate in bits per second which is known as baud rate. Examples of baud rate for communicating with the computer may include 300, 600, 1200, 2400, 4800, 9600, 14400, 19200, 28800, 38400, 57600, or 115200. A universal asynchronous receiver/transmitter (UART) is responsible for implementing serial communication. UART acts as an intermediate between serial and parallel interface. All Arduino boards have at least one serial port (also known as a UART or USART. The RF modem and GSM modem are two modules, works on serial communication.

Keywords: 2.4GHz, Arduino, GSM.

3.1. SERIAL COMMUNICATION WITH 2.4 GHZ RF MODEM

This section describes the serial communication with RF modem with 2.4 GHz frequency. The complete system comprises two sections transmitter and receiver. Transmitter section comprises Arduino Nano, power supply, LCD (20x4), temperature sensor, MQ135 sensor, and 2.4GHz RF modem. Receiver section comprises of Arduino Nano, power supply, LCD (20x4) and RF modem. The system has been designed so that mobile platform can be controlled wirelessly, with the help of 2.4 GHz RF modem. Fig. (**3.1**) shows the block diagram of the transmitter section and Fig. (**3.2**) shows the block diagram of the receiver section.

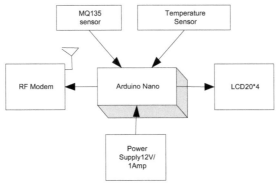

Fig. (3.1). Block diagram of the transmitter section.

Rajesh Singh, Anita Gehlot & Bhupendra Singh

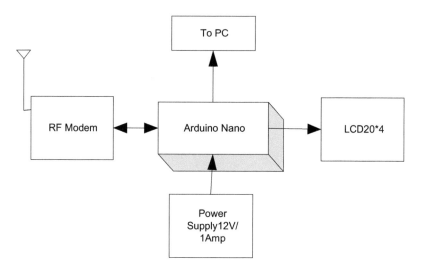

Fig. (3.2). Block diagram of the receiver section.

Table **3.1** describes the components list, required to develop the transmitter section. Table **3.2** describes the components list, required to develop the receiver section.

Table 3.1. Component list for transmitter section.

Components	Quality
Power Supply 12V/500mA	1
+12V to 5V converter	1
Power supply patch/ breakout	1
Arduino Nano	1
MQ135 sensor	1
LED	1
330 ohm resistor	1
LCD16*4	1
LCD patch/ breakout board for 16*4	1
M-F connector jumper wire	20
F-F connector jumper wire	20
M-M connector jumper wire	20
Temperature sensor	1
2.4 GHz RF modem	1
RF modem patch	1

Table 3.2. Component list for receiver section.

Components	Quality
Power Supply 12V/500mA	1
+12V to 5V converter	1
Power supply patch/ breakout	1
Arduino Nano	1
LED	1
330 ohm resistor	1
LCD16*4	1
LCD patch/ breakout board for 16*4	1
M-F connector jumper wire	20
F-F connector jumper wire	20
M-M connector jumper wire	20
2.4 GHz RF modem	1
RF modem patch	1

Note: All components are available at www.nuttyengineer.com

2.4GHz RF Modem

2.4 GHz RF modem is a reliable module, which can transfer serial data. It enables bi-directional communication for wireless data communication. It works in half duplex mode with the facility of automatic switching of transmitter and receiver mode. It can receive/transmit data at the baud rate of 9600/115200 bps. It can operate on 5V or 3V DC, for direct interfacing with microcontroller. Fig. (**3.3**) shows the view of 2.4GHz RF modem.

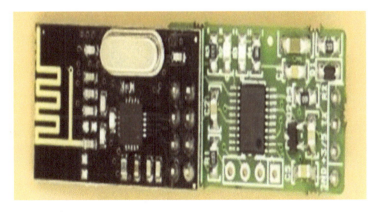

Fig. (3.3). 2.4 GHz RF modem.

This modem has self-controlled communication protocol with complete transparency to user interface, which makes it most useful and easy to handle device.

3.1.1. Circuit Diagram

The section 3.1.1.1 and section 3.1.1.2 describe the interfacing connections of transmitter and receiver section, respectively.

3.1.1.1. Circuit Diagram of Transmitter Section

Fig. (**3.4**) shows the circuit diagram of the transmitter section. The circuit shows the connections with MQ135 sensor, temperature sensor, LCD/LED, Arduino Nano, RF modem and power supply 12V/1Amp.

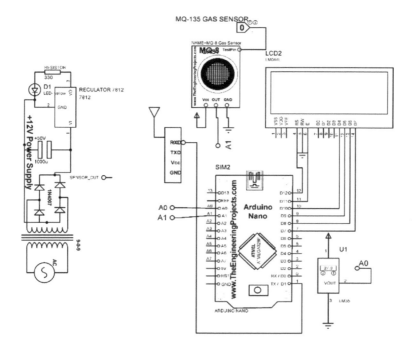

Fig. (3.4). Circuit of transmitter section.

The connections are as follows-

1. +12V and GND (ground) pin of power adaptor are connected with female DC jack of the Arduino Nano respectively.
2. +5V and GND (ground) pin of the power supply are connected to +5V and

GND pin of LCD patch/ breakout board respectively.

3. RS, RW and E control pins of LCD patch/ breakout board are connected to D12, GND, D11 pins of Arduino Nano board respectively.

4. D4, D5, D6, D7 pins of LCD patch/ breakout board are connected to D10, D9, D8, D7 pins of Arduino Nano respectively.

5. +Vcc, GND, OUT pins of MQ135 sensor are connected to +5V, GND, A1 pins of Arduino Nano respectively.

6. +Vcc, GND, OUT pins of Temperature sensor are connected to +5V, GND, A0 pins of Arduino Nano respectively.

7. +Vcc, GND, RX pins of RF modem are connected to +5V, GND and TX pin of Arduino Nano.

3.1.1.2. Circuit Diagram of Receiver Section

Fig. (**3.5**) shows the circuit diagram of the receiver section. The circuit shows the interfacing connection among LCD/LED, Arduino Nano, RF modem and power supply 12V/1Amp.

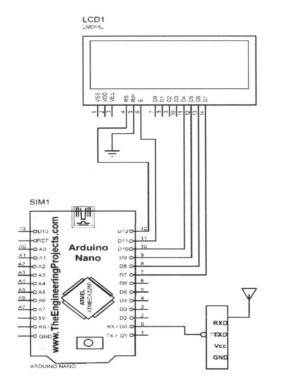
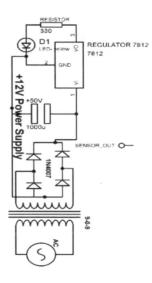

Fig. (3.5). Circuit of receiver section.

The connections are as follows-

1. +12V and GND (ground) pin of power adaptor is connected with female DC jack of the Arduino Nano respectively.
2. The +5V and GND (ground) pin of the power supply is connected to +5V and GND pin of LCD patch/ breakout board respectively.
3. RS, RW and E control pins of LCD patch/ breakout board are connected to D12, GND, D11 pins of Arduino Nano board respectively.
4. D4, D5, D6, D7 pins of LCD patch/ breakout board are connected to D10, D9, D8, D7 pins of Arduino Nano respectively.
5. +Vcc, GND, TX pins of RF modem is connected to +5V, GND and RX pin of Arduino Nano.

3.1.2. Program Code

The section 3.1.2.1 and section 3.1.2.2 shows the program for transmitter and receiver section respectively.

3.1.2.1. Transmitter Program

```
const int Touch_sensor_pin = A0; // connect touch sensor to A0 pin

int Touch_sensor_state=0; // assign state

///////// for Air quality sensor

int MQ135_sensor_pin=A1; // connect MQ135 sensor to A1 pin

int MQ135_sensor_level=0; // assign state

#include <LiquidCrystal.h> // add LCD library

LiquidCrystal lcd (12, 11, 10, 9, 8, 7); // connect pins of LCD with Arduino Nano

void setup()

{

lcd.begin(20,4);// Initialize LCD

Serial.begin(9600);// initialize Serial communication

pinMode (Touch_sensor_pin, INPUT_PULLUP);// make pin A0 as active LOW input
```

```
}

void loop()

{

Touch_sensor_state = digitalRead (Touch_sensor_pin);//read vibration sensor as
digital input

MQ135_sensor_level=analogRead (MQ135_sensor_pin);// read MQ135 sensor as
analog input

if(Touch_sensor_state == LOW) // check state

{

lcd.clear(); // clear LCD

int Touch_sensor_variable=10; // assume touch sensor status is 10 at True
condition

lcd.setCursor(0,0); // set cursor of LCD

lcd.print("TOUCH STATUS:"); // print string on LCD

lcd.setCursor(0,1); // set cursor of LCD

lcd.print("Yes"); // print string on LCD

lcd.setCursor(0,2); // set cursor on LCD

lcd.print("GAS_Level:"); // print string on LCD

lcd.setCursor(0,3); // set cursor on LCD

lcd.print(MQ135_sensor_level); // print the level of MQ135 sensor on LCD

Serial.print(Touch_sensor_variable); // send variable data on serial

Serial.print(":"); // print string on LCD

Serial.print(MQ135_sensor_level); // serial print the data od MQ135

Serial.print('\r'); // print end character on serial

delay(50); // wait for 50mSec
```

```
}
```

else

```
{
```

lcd.clear(); // clear previous contents from LCD

int Touch_sensor_variable=20; // assume touch sensor status is 20 at false condition

lcd.setCursor(0,0); // set cursor on LCD

lcd.print("TOUCH STATUS:"); // print string on LCD

lcd.setCursor(0,1); // set cursor on LCD

lcd.print("Yes"); // print string on LCD

lcd.setCursor(0,2); // set cursor on LCD

lcd.print("MQ135_Level:");

lcd.setCursor(0,3); // set cursor on LCD

lcd.print(MQ135_sensor_level); // print value of MQ135 sensor on LCD

Serial.print(Touch_sensor_variable); // print serial the value of digital sensor

Serial.print(":"); // print string on serial

Serial.print(MQ135_sensor_level); // print serial the value of MQ135 sensor

Serial.print('\r'); // print end character on serial

delay(50); // wait for 50 mSec }

```
}
```

3.1.2.2. Receiver Program

#include <LiquidCrystal.h> // add LCD library

LiquidCrystal lcd(12, 11, 10, 9, 8, 7); // connect pins of LCD on Arduino nano

String inputString_arduino = ""; // assume string

```
boolean Arduino_stringComplete = false; // take digital varaibale

int TOUCH_sensor_level,MQ135_sensor_level; // variable of vibration sensor

void setup()

{

lcd.begin(20,4); // initialize LCD

Serial.begin(9600); // initialize serial communication

inputString_arduino.reserve(200); // reserver string of 200 byte

}

void loop()

{

arduino_serialEvent(); // call function to read serial data from transmitter side

if(TOUCH_sensor_level == 10) // check state

{

lcd.clear(); // clear LCD

lcd.setCursor(0,0); // set cursor on LCD

lcd.print("TOUCH STATUS:"); // print string on LCD

lcd.setCursor(0,1); // set cursor on LCD

lcd.print ("Yes"); // print string on LCD

lcd.setCursor (0,2); // set cursor on LCD

lcd.print ("GAS_ Level:"); // print string on LCD

lcd.setCursor (0,3); // set cursor on LCD

lcd.print (MQ135_sensor_level); // print MQ6 sensor level

delay(50); // wait for 50 mSec

}
```

else if (TOUCH_sensor_level == 20)

{

lcd.clear (); // clear LCD

lcd.setCursor (0,0); // set cursor on LCD

lcd.print ("TOUCH STATUS:"); // print string on LCD

lcd.setCursor (0,1); // set cursor on LCD

lcd.print ("NO "); // print string on LCD

lcd.setCursor (0,2); // set cursor on LCD

lcd.print ("GAS _Level:"); // print string on LCD

lcd.setCursor (0,3); // set cursor on LCD

lcd.print (MQ135_sensor_level);// print value on LCD

delay (50); // wait for 50 mSec

} }

void arduino_serialEvent () // function to read serial value from transmitter section

{

while (Serial.available()>0) // che ck serial data greater than 1

{

char BYTE_serial = (char) Serial.read (); // read serial data

inputString_arduino += BYTE_serial; // store data in string

if (BYTE_serial == '\r') // if last byte is then terminate

{

TOUCH_sensor_level=(((inputString_arduino[0]-48)*10)+((inputString_arduino[1]-48)*1));

MQ135_sensor_level=(((inputString_arduino[3]-

48)*100)+((inputString_arduino[4]-48)*10)+((inputString_arduino[5]-48)*1));/// only 3 byte can be received for MQ6

}

}

}

3.2. SERIAL COMMUNICATION WITH GSM MODEM

This section describes the serial communication with GSM modem. The system comprises of Arduino Nano, GSM modem, LCD (20x4), power supply and personal computer (to see data serially), mobile phone. The objective of the system is to demonstrate the working of GSM modem. It can also read the message from mobile phone as receiver. Fig. (**3.6**) shows the block diagram of the system.

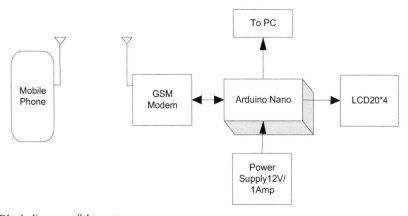

Fig. (3.6). Block diagram of the system.

Table **3.3** describes the components list, required to develop the system.

Table 3.3. Component list.

Components	Quality
Power Supply 12V/500mA	1
+12V to 5V converter	1
Power supply patch/ breakout	1
Arduino Nano	1
LED	1

(Table 3.3) cont.....

Components	Quality
330 ohm resistor	1
LCD16*4	1
LCD patch/ breakout board for 16*4	1
M-F connector jumper wire	20
F-F connector jumper wire	20
M-M connector jumper wire	20
GSM modem	1

Note: All components are available at www.nuttyengineer.com

3.2.1. Circuit Diagram

Fig. (**3.7**) shows the circuit diagram of the system. The circuit shows the interfacing connection between LCD/LED, Arduino Nano, GSM modem and power supply 12V/1Amp.

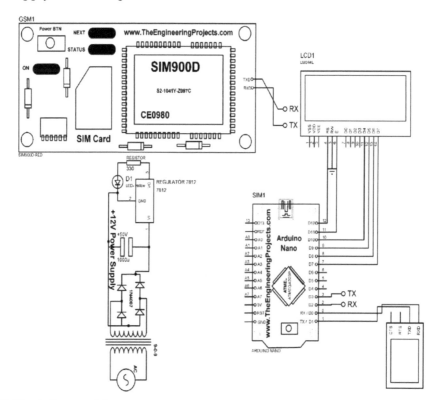

Fig. (3.7). Circuit diagram of the system.

The connections are as follows-

1. +12V and GND (ground) pin of power adaptor are connected with female DC jack of the Arduino Nano respectively.
2. The +5V and GND (ground) pin of the power supply are connected to +5V and GND pin of LCD patch/ breakout board respectively.
3. RS, RW and E control pins of LCD patch/ breakout board are connected to D12, GND, D11 pins of Arduino Nano board respectively.
4. D4, D5, D6, D7 pins of LCD patch/ breakout board are connected to D10. D9, D8, D7 pins of Arduino Nano respectively.
5. +Vcc, GND, RX, TX pins of GSM modem are connected to +5V, GND TX and RX pin of Arduino Nano respectively.

3.2.2. Program Code

```
#include <LiquidCrystal.h> // add library of LCD

LiquidCrystal lcd(12, 11, 10, 9, 8,7); // connect pins of LCD to Arduino Nano

////// softserial library to make pin 2 as RX and 3pin as TX

#include <SoftwareSerial.h> // add soft serial library for GSM to create RX and TX

SoftwareSerial rajSerial(2, 3); // pin 2 is RX and pin 3 is TX in Arduino Nano

void setup()

{

rajSerial.begin(9600); // Set the GSM baud rate 9600

Serial.begin(9600); // Serial monitor Baud rate 9600

delay(100); // set delay of 100 mSec

lcd.setCursor(0,0); // set cursor on LCD

lcd.begin(20,4); // initialize LCD

lcd.setCursor(0,0); // set cursor on LCD

lcd.print("GSM system to"); // print string on LCD

lcd.setCursor(0,1); // set cursor on LCD
```

```
lcd.print("Send and receive"); // print string on LCD

lcd.setCursor(0,2); // set cursor on LCD

lcd.print("at UPES"); // print string on LCD

delay(2000); // wait for 2 Sec

lcd.clear(); // clear LCD

}

void loop()

{

if (Serial.available()>0) // check serial communication greater than 0

switch(Serial.read()) // switch to serial

{

case 'S': // case S

SendMessage_form_GSM_MODEM();// send message using GSM

break; // break case

case 'R': // case R

RecieveMessage_form_GSM_MODEM(); // recive message from GSM

break; // break case

}

if (rajSerial.available()>0) // check serial communication greater than 0

Serial.write(rajSerial.read()); // print serial data which read by serial

}

void SendMessage_form_GSM_MODEM() // function to send message

{

rajSerial.println("AT+CMGF=1"); // GSM modem in Text mode
```

delay(1000); // wait for 1 Sec

rajSerial.println("AT+CMGS=\"mobile no.\"\r"); //set mobile where u want to send SMS

delay(1000); // wait for 1 Sec

rajSerial.println("MESSAGE FROM GSM MODEM AT UPES");// TEXT message as you wish

delay(100); // wait for 100 mSec

rajSerial.println((char)26);// ASCII code of CTRL+Z

delay(1000); // // wait for 1 Sec

lcd.setCursor(0,1); // set cursor on LCD

lcd.print("Message completed"); // print string on LCD

}

void RecieveMessage_form_GSM_MODEM() // function to receive message from mobile

{

rajSerial.println("AT+CNMI=2,2,0,0,0"); // AT Command to receive a live SMS

lcd.setCursor(0,2); // set cursor on LCD

lcd.print("RECEIVED MESSAGE"); // print string on LCD

delay(1000); //// wait for 1 Sec

}

CHAPTER 4

Introduction to Scilab and GUI without Toolbox

Abstract: Scilab is an open source, cross-platform numerical computational package with a high-level, numerically oriented programming language. It can be used for signal and image processing, statistical analysis, internet of things, data mining, *etc.*

A Graphic User Interface (GUI) is a graphical display, which comprises devices, or components, to make the user enable to perform interactive tasks. To design a GUI, the user need not create a script or type commands at the command line. The GUI components include menus, toolbars, push buttons, radio buttons, list boxes, sliders, *etc.* In SCILAB, a GUI can be used to display data in tabular form or as plots. The SCILAB graphical user interface development environment provides a set of tools for creating graphical user interfaces (GUIs). These tools are used to simplify the process of laying out and programming GUIs. This chapter gives a brief introduction to Scilab and step wise description to GUI without toolbox.

Keywords: GUI, Scilab.

4.1. SCILAB GUI

Steps to design GUI in Scilab

1. Download GUI Builder and copy it in 'contrib' folder of Scilab in the 'C' drive.
2. Install GUI Builder in the Scilab.
3. Download Scilab-Serial-master library and place inside 'contrib' folder of Scilab in the C drive.
4. Write guibuilder command in the main window of Scilab. Then a window will open, as shown in Figs. (**4.1**, **4.2**) shows snapshot of blank window.
5. Click on pushbutton. Then a new window will open to write the 'Tag' and 'String' name on it as shown in Fig. (**4.3**).
6. Repeat the process to make the other pushbutton in the window as per the requirement of the project.
7. The position, width and height of pushbutton can also be changed, using the facility in the left window of guibuilder as shown in Fig. (**4.4**).

Fig. (4.1). snapshot Guibuilder window.

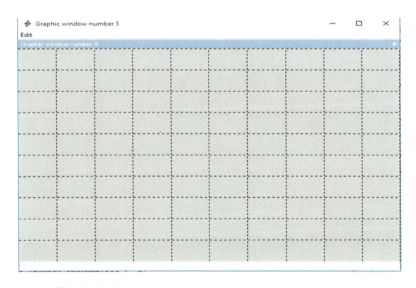

Fig. (4.2). Snapshot of blank window.

Fig (4.3). Snapshot of window to write the 'Tag' and 'String' name.

Fig. (4.4). Snapshot of window to change the position, width and height of pushbutton.

8. After creating the GUI, click on generate option in the left window of guibuilder and save the GUI, by writing appropriate name as shown in Fig. (**4.5**).

9. A .sce file will open, where components occur (as per the blocks in GUI created). *e.g.* GUI for robot may have following components.

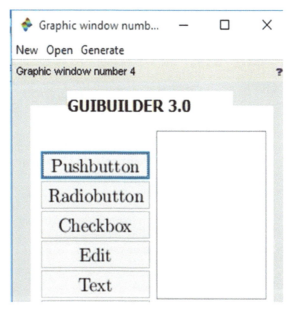

Fig. (4.5). Snapshot to generate option in left window of guibuilder.

function FORWARD_callback (handles), function REVERSE_callback (handles), function LEFT_callback (handles), function RIGHT_callback (handles) and function STOP_callback(handles).

1. Inside the functions, write three commands-

function <u>FORWARD_callback</u> (**handles**)

h=<u>openserial</u>(1,"9600,n,8,1");

<u>writeserial</u>(h,"a");

<u>closeserial</u>(h);

endfunction

2. Similarly write commands for all functions and GUI is ready to communicate with Arduino.

Write program in Arduino to receive commands from Scilab GUI.

CHAPTER 5

Scilab Arduino_1.1 Package (using toolbox_ arduino_v3.ino)

Abstract: This chapter describes the steps to get started with the Scilab XCOS package for the Arduino. One of the popular methods to control the Arduino with Scilab is with the help of the Arduino_1.1 package. In this method there is no need to write a program to receive commands from Scilab, instead a predefined package is installed in the Arduino and then with the help of XCOS scilab GUI is created. XCOS is a package from Scilab which is used for modelling and simulation of the system. It is an open source Simulink and helpful to create Simulink models. XCOS is a graphical editor to design a hybrid systems model. Models can be designed, loaded, saved, compiled and simulated.

Keywords: Arduino_1.1 package, Scilab.

5.1. STEPS TO INSTALL PACKAGE IN ARDUINO

1. **Step-1:** Download and install Scilab.
2. **Step-2:** Download the Arduino toolbox from toolbox_arduino_v3.ino and connect the Arduino board to the PC/laptop through the serial port.
3. **Step-3:** Open the Arduino IDE and upload the sketch toolbox_arduino_v3.ino to the Arduino.
4. **Step-4:** Download the Arduino_1.1 package and paste it in the 'contrib' folder with path C:\Program Files (x86)\scilab-5.5.2.
5. **Step-5:** Go to the 'contrib' folder and then to the Arduino_1.1 folder and run 'loader.sce' file, to install Arduino in Scilab XCOS.
6. **Step-6:** Open XCOS by clicking on the icon in the Scilab window, as shown in Fig. (**5.1**).
7. **Step-7:** Click on XCOS to open a palette window with the Arduino folder, as shown in Fig. (**5.2**). In the Arduino folder, there are different building blocks to design the GUI.

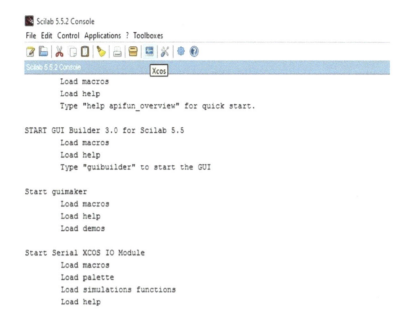

Fig. (5.1). Snapshot of window to open 'XCOS'.

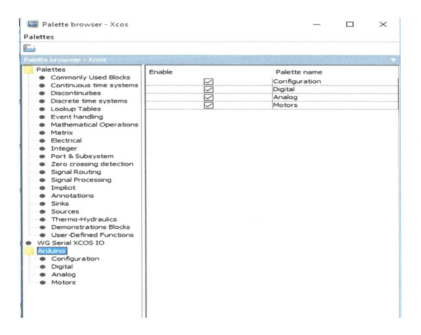

Fig. (5.2). Snapshot of palette window in XCOS.

5.2. BLOCKS OF SCILAB XCOS

This section discusses the basic building blocks used to design a GUI (Graphical User Interface). The GUI can be designed by adding the building blocks to the untitled space and then assigning the values as per the requirement of the project.

Building Blocks of XCOS:

1. **Arduino_Setup** – Double click on it, then assign a comport number to this block which is identified on connecting the Arduino to the PC/laptop, as shown in Fig. (**5.3**).
2. **Time_Sample** – Double click on it, and set the sample time of the Arduino, as shown in (Fig. **5.4**).
3. **Digital_Read** – Double click on it, then data from any digital pin of Arduino can be read, Fig. (**5.5**).
4. **Digital_Write** – Double click on it, then assign this digital pin as 'High' or 'Low', as shown in Fig. (**5.6**).
5. **Analog_Read** – Double click on it, then data from any analog pin of the Arduino can be read, as shown in Fig. (**5.7**).
    1. **Analog_Write** – Double click on it, then any analog pin of the Arduino can be assigned the value, as shown in Fig. (**5.8**).
    2. **Servo_Write** – Double click on it, then angle value to servo can be assigned to the pin of the Arduino, where servo is connected, as shown in Fig. (**5.9**).

Fig. (**5.3**). Arduino_Setup.

Fig. (**5.4**). Time_Sample.

Fig. (5.5). Digital_Read.

Fig. (5.6). Digital_Write.

Fig. (5.7). Analog_Read.

Fig. (5.8). Analog_write.

Fig. (5.9). Servo_write.

5.3. DIGITAL READ

This section describes the method to read a digital sensor using the Arduino and Scilab XCOS model with the help of a simple example of reading a fire sensor.

Fig. (**5.10**) shows the block diagram of the system. The system comprises the power supply, an Arduino Uno and a fire sensor. The objective is to read the fire/flame sensor as the digital sensor and communicate the status of the sensor to Scilab XCOS, using a serial link with the Arduino I/O package.

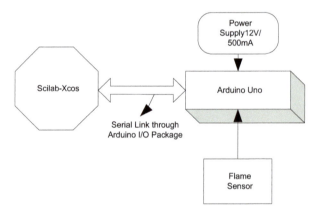

Fig. (5.10). Block diagram of the system.

Table **5.1** describes the component list required to develop the system.

Table 5.1. Component list.

Component/ Device	Quality
Power Supply 12V/500mA	1
+12V to 5V converter	1

(Table 5.1) cont.....

Component/ Device	Quality
Power supply patch/ breakout	1
Arduino Uno	1
Fire sensor	1
M-F connector jumper wire	20
F-F connector jumper wire	20
M-M connector jumper wire	20
PC/Laptop with Scilab XCOS	1

Note: All components are available at www.nuttyengineer.com

5.3.1. Circuit Diagram

The connections of the circuit are as follows-

1. +12V and GND (ground) pins of the power adaptor are connected with female DC jack of the Arduino Uno.
2. +Vcc, GND, OUT pins of a fire sensor are connected to +5V, GND, D6 pins of the Arduino Uno respectively.
3. Add the basic blocks to Scilab XCOS, as shown in Fig. (**5.12**).
4. Load the package to the Arduino and check the working of the system.

Fig. (**5.11**) shows circuit diagram of the interfacing of fire sensor with Arduino.

Fig. (**5.13**) shows the output waveform of the designed system.

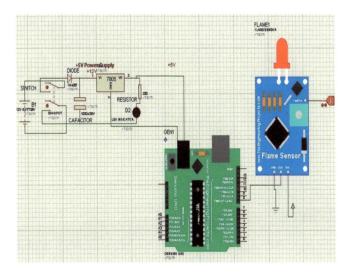

Fig. (5.11). Circuit diagram of the interfacing of fire sensor with Arduino.

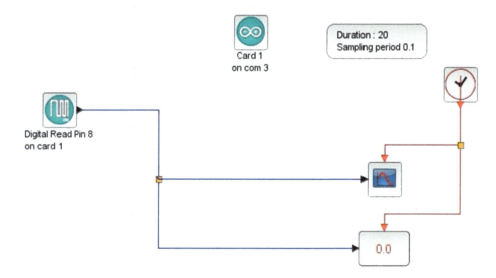

Fig. (5.12). XCOS Model to read a digital sensor.

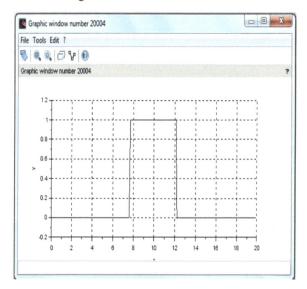

Fig. (5.13). Digital sensor waveform.

5.4. DIGITAL WRITE

This section describes the method to write an Arduino digital pin connected to Scilab XCOS model, with the help of a simple example of changing status of a LED.

Fig. (**5.14**) shows the block diagram of the system. The system comprises of a power supply, an Arduino Uno and a LED. The objective is to change the status of a LED connected to digital pin of the Arduino with Scilab XCOS, using a serial link with the Arduino I/O package.

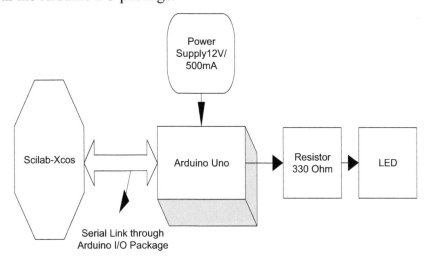

Fig. (5.14). Block diagram of the system.

Table **5.2** describes the component list, required to develop the system.

Table 5.2. Component list.

Component/ Device	Quality
Power Supply 12V/500mA	1
+12V to 5V converter	1
Power supply patch/ breakout	1
Arduino Uno	1
LED	1
M-F connector jumper wire	20
F-F connector jumper wire	20
M-M connector jumper wire	20
PC/Laptop with Scilab XCOS	1

Note: All components are available at www.nuttyengineer.com

5.4.1. Circuit Diagram

The connections of circuit are as follows-

1. +12V and GND (ground) pins of the power adaptor are connected with female DC jack of the Arduino Uno.
2. Anode terminal of a LED is connected to D4 pin of the Arduino Uno through a resistor and cathode terminal to GND (Ground).
3. Add the basic blocks to Scilab XCOS, as shown in Fig. (**5.16**).
4. Load the package to Arduino and check the working of the system.

Fig. (**5.15**) shows circuit diagram of the interfacing of LED with Arduino.

Fig. (**5.17**) shows the output waveform of the designed system.

5.5. DIGITAL READ AND WRITE

This section describes the method to read and write digital data to an Arduino digital pin using Scilab XCOS model, with the help of a simple example of changing the status of LED with respect to the change in status of a flame sensor.

Fig. (**5.18**) shows the block diagram of the system. The system comprises of a power supply, an Arduino Uno, a flame sensor and a LED. The objective is to demonstrate the digital read and write process, with Scilab XCOS, using a serial link with the Arduino I/O package.

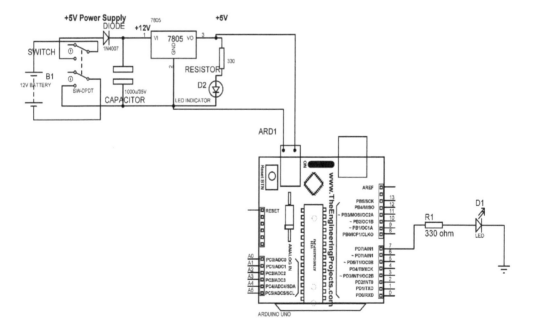

Fig. (5.15). Circuit diagram of the interfacing of LED with Arduino.

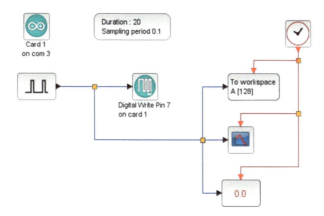

Fig. (5.16). XCOS model to write digital sensor.

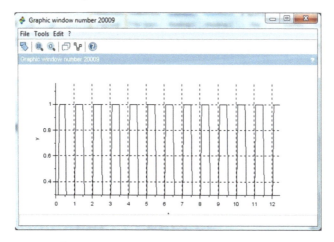

Fig. (5.17). Digital sensor waveform.

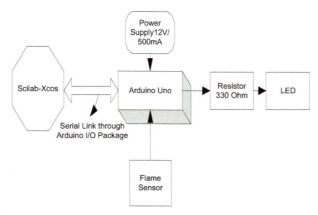

Fig. (5.18). Block diagram of the system.

Table **5.3** describes the component list, required to develop the system.

Table 5.3. Component list.

Component/ Device	Quality
Power Supply 12V/500mA	1
+12V to 5V converter	1
Power supply patch/ breakout	1
Arduino Uno	1
LED	1
Flame sensor	1
Flame sensor patch	1
M-F connector jumper wire	20
F-F connector jumper wire	20
M-M connector jumper wire	20
PC/Laptop with Scilab XCOS	1

Note: All components are available at www.nuttyengineer.com

5.5.1. Circuit Diagram

The connections of the circuit are as follows-

1. +12V and GND (ground) pins of the power adaptor are connected with female DC jack of the Arduino Uno.
2. Anode terminal of a LED is connected to D4 pin of the Arduino Uno through a resistor and cathode terminal to GND (Ground).
3. +Vcc, GND, OUT pins of a fire sensor are connected to +5V, GND, D8 pins of the Arduino Uno respectively.
4. Add the basic blocks to Scilab XCOS, as shown in Fig. (**5.20**).
5. Load the package to Arduino and check the working of the system.

Fig. (**5.19**) shows circuit diagram of the interfacing of fire sensor and LED with Arduino.

Fig. (**5.21**) shows the output waveform of the designed system.

5.6. ANALOG READ WITH POTENTIOMETER

This section describes the method to read an analog sensor using Arduino and Scilab XCOS model, with the help of a simple example of reading 10K Potentiometer.

Fig. (**5.22**) shows the block diagram of the system. The system comprises of a power supply, an Arduino Nano and a 10K POT. The objective is to read the potentiometer as an analog sensor and communicate the status of the sensor to Scilab XCOS, using a serial link with the Arduino I/O package.

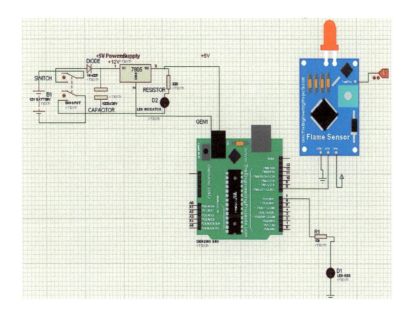

Fig. (5.19). Circuit diagram of the interfacing of fire sensor and LED with Arduino.

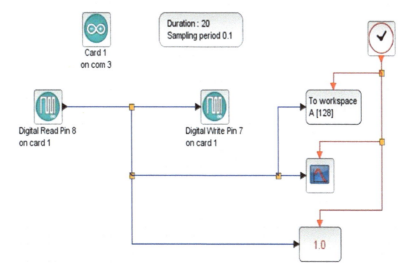

Fig. (5.20). XCOS Model for digital read/ write.

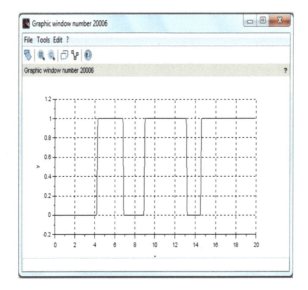

Fig. (5.21). Digital read/ write waveform.

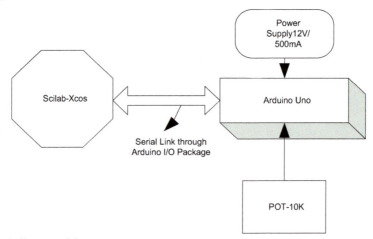

Fig. (5.22). Block diagram of the system.

Table **5.4** describes the component list, required to develop the system.

Table 5.4. Component list.

Component/ Device	Quality
Power Supply 12V/500mA	1
+12V to 5V converter	1
Power supply patch/ breakout	1

(Table 5.4) cont.....

Component/ Device	Quality
Arduino Uno	1
10K Potentiometer	1
M-F connector jumper wire	20
F-F connector jumper wire	20
M-M connector jumper wire	20
PC/Laptop with Scilab XCOS	1

Note: All components are available at www.nuttyengineer.com

5.6.1. Circuit Diagram

The connections of the circuit are as follows-

1. +12V and GND (ground) pins of the power adaptor are connected with female DC jack of the Arduino Uno.
2. +Vcc, GND, OUT pins of a POT are connected to +5V, GND, A0 pin (analog read pin 0) of the Arduino Uno respectively.
3. Add the basic blocks to Scilab XCOS, as shown in Fig. (**5.24**).
4. Load the package to the Arduino and check the working of the system.

Fig. (**5.23**) shows circuit diagram of the interfacing of POT with Arduino.

Fig. (**5.25**) shows the output waveform of the designed system.

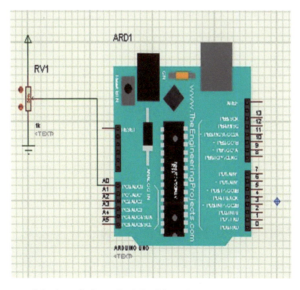

Fig. (5.23). Circuit diagram of the interfacing of POT with Arduino.

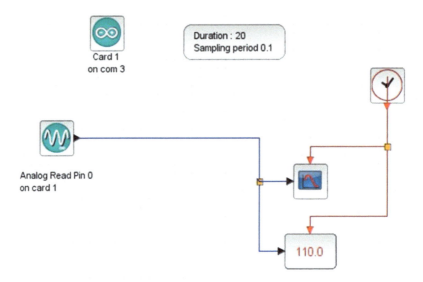

Fig. (5.24). XCOS Model for analog read.

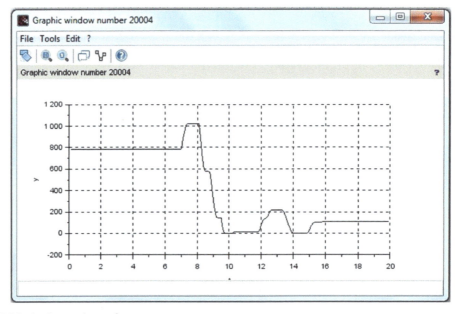

Fig. (5.25). Analog read waveform.

5.7. ANALOG READ WITH TEMPERATURE SENSOR

This section describes the method to read an analog sensor using the Arduino and Scilab XCOS model, with the help of a simple example of reading a temperature sensor.

Fig. (**5.26**) shows the block diagram of the system. The block diagram of the system comprises of a power supply, an Arduino Uno and a temperature sensor (LM35). The objective is to read LM35 as analog sensor and communicate the status of the sensor to Scilab XCOS, using a serial link with the Arduino I/O package.

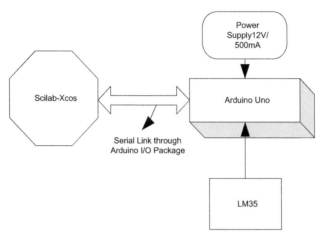

Fig. (5.26). Block diagram of the system.

Table **5.5** describes the component list, required to develop the system.

Table 5.5. Component list.

Component/ Device	Quality
Power Supply 12V/500mA	1
+12V to 5V converter	1
Power supply patch/ breakout	1
Arduino Uno	1
LM35	1
M-F connector jumper wire	20
F-F connector jumper wire	20
M-M connector jumper wire	20
PC/Laptop with Scilab XCOS	1

Note: All components are available at www.nuttyengineer.com

5.7.1. Circuit Diagram

The connections of circuit are as follows-

1. +12V and GND (ground) pins of the power adaptor is connected with female DC jack of the Arduino Uno.
2. +Vcc, GND, OUT pins of a LM35 sensor are connected to +5V, GND, A0 pin (analog read pin 0) of the Arduino Uno respectively.
3. Add the basic blocks to SCilab XCOS, as shown in Fig. (**5.28**).
4. Load the package to Arduino and check the working of the system.

Fig. (**5.27**) shows circuit diagram of the interfacing of temperature sensor with Arduino.

Fig. (**5.29**) shows an analog read waveform.

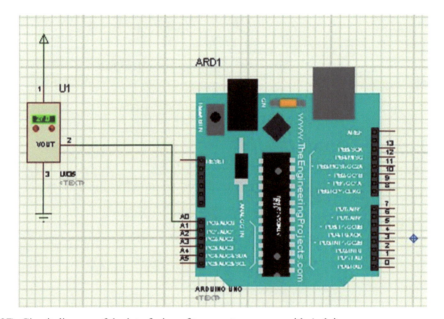

Fig. (5.27). Circuit diagram of the interfacing of temperature sensor with Arduino.

5.8. ANALOG READ WRITE

This section describes the method to read and write an analog signal, using the Arduino and Scilab XCOS model, with the help of a simple example of changing the status of a LED with respect to change in status of temperature sensor.

Fig. (**5.30**) shows the block diagram of the system. The system comprises of a power supply, an Arduino Uno, a temperature sensor (LM35) and a LED. The objective is to read and write an analog signal with Scilab XCOS, using a serial link with the Arduino I/O package.

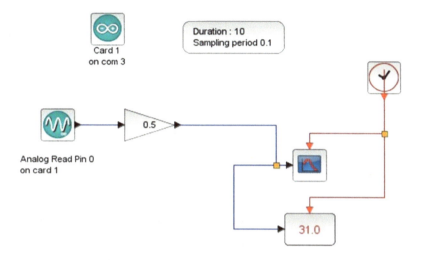

Fig. (5.28). XCOS Model for analog read0.

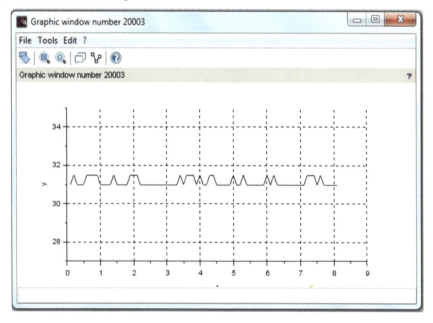

Fig. (5.29). Analog read waveform.

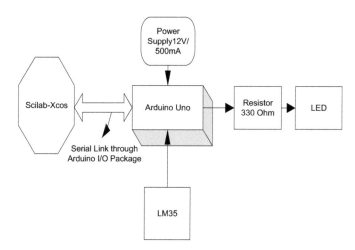

Fig. (5.30). Block diagram of the system.

Table **5.6** describes the component list, required to develop the system.

Table 5.6. Component list.

Component/ Device	Quality
Power Supply 12V/500mA	1
+12V to 5V converter	1
Power supply patch/ breakout	1
Arduino Uno	1
LED	1
Temperature sensor (LM35)	1
M-F connector jumper wire	20
F-F connector jumper wire	20
M-M connector jumper wire	20
PC/Laptop with Scilab XCOS	1

Note: All components are available at www.nuttyengineer.com

5.8.1. Circuit Diagram

The connections of circuit are as follows-

1. +12V and GND (ground) pins of the power adaptor is connected with female DC jack of the Arduino Uno.
2. +Vcc, GND, OUT pins of a LM35 are connected to +5V, GND, A0 pin (analog

read pin 0) of the Arduino Uno respectively.
3. Anode terminal of a LED is connected to D3 pin (PWM as analog write pin) of the Arduino Uno through a resistor and cathode terminal to GND (Ground).
4. Add the basic blocks to Scilab XCOS, as shown in Fig. (**5.32**).
5. Load the package to Arduino and check the working of the system.

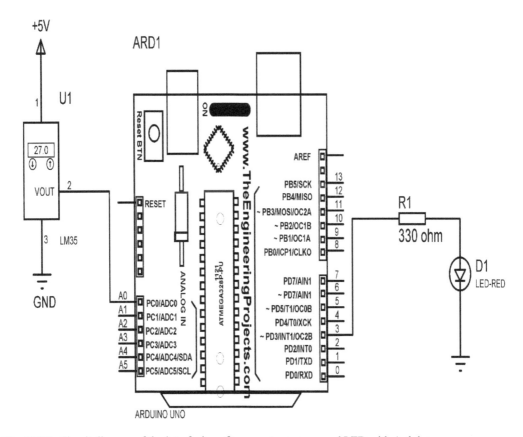

Fig. (5.31). Circuit diagram of the interfacing of temperature sensor and LED with Arduino.

Fig. (**5.31**) shows circuit diagram of the interfacing of temperature sensor and LED with Arduino

Fig. (**5.33**) shows the output waveform of the designed system.

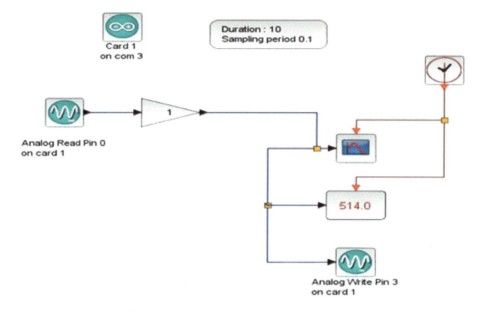

Fig. (5.32). XCOS Model for analog read/write.

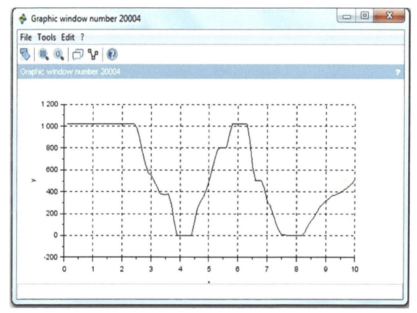

Fig. (5.33). Analog read/write waveform.

CHAPTER 6

Servo Motor Control with Arduino_1.1 Package

Abstract: A servomotor is an actuator which provides precise control of angular or linear position. It consists of a motor and a sensor for taking feedback. The servo motor is combination of four things: a DC motor, a gear reduction unit, a position-sensing device and a control circuit. The servo motor can be used for high technology like automation. Servos can be used in elevators, rudders, walking a robot, or operating grippers. The motor can be controlled with a PWM (pulse width modulator) signal. This chapter discusses the working of servo motor with respect to change in light intensity sensed by LDR, with the help of Scilab XCOS and Arduino I/O package.

Keywords: Arduino_1.1 package, Scilab.

To understand the read/write operations with Scilab XCOS, a system is designed to control servo motor. The angle of servo motor changes with respect to change in light intensity sensed with LDR. Fig. (**6.1**) shows the block diagram of the system. The block diagram comprises power supply, Arduino Uno, LDR (Light Dependent Resistor) sensor and servo motor. The objective of the system is to read the LDR sensor connected to analog pin and with respect to status of sensor, write the data to digital pin (PWM pin) of Arduino Uno, using Scilab XCOS and serial link (Arduino I/O package).

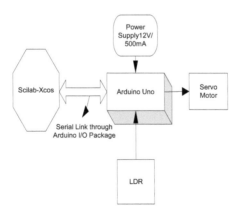

Fig. (6.1). Block diagram of the System.

Rajesh Singh, Anita Gehlot & Bhupendra Singh

Table **6.1** describes the components list, required to develop the system.

Table 6.1. Component list

Components/ Device	Quality
Power Supply 12V/500mA	1
+12V to 5V converter	1
Power supply patch/ breakout	1
Arduino Uno	1
LDR	1
Servo motor	1
M-F connector jumper wire	20
F-F connector jumper wire	20
M-M connector jumper wire	20
PC/Laptop with Scilab XCOS	1

Note: All components are available at www.nuttyengineer.com

Light Dependent Resistor (LDR) is also known as a cadmium sulfide (CdS) cell or photo resistor. It is also called a photoconductor. It works on the principle of photoconductivity. The resistance of passive component decreases, if the light intensity decreases. This device can be used to identify light or dark in switching circuits. Fig. (**6.2**) shows the view of LDR sensor.

Fig. (6.2). LDR sensor from nuttyengineer.com.

6.1. CIRCUIT DIAGRAM

Fig. (**6.3**) shows the circuit diagram of the system. The circuit shows the interfacing connection of LDR, servo motor, Arduino Uno and power supply.

The connections are as follows-

1. +12V and GND (ground) pin of power adaptor is connected with female DC jack of the Arduino Uno respectively.
2. +Vcc, GND, OUT pins of light dependent resistor (LDR) sensor are connected to +5V, GND, A0 pin (analog read pin 0) of Arduino Uno respectively.
3. Connect +Vcc, GND and pulse pins of servo to +5V, GND and pin3 (PWM) of the Arduino Uno respectively.
4. Add the basic blocks to Scilab XCOS, as per requirement, as shown in Fig. (**6.4**).
5. Load the package to Arduino and check the working of the system.

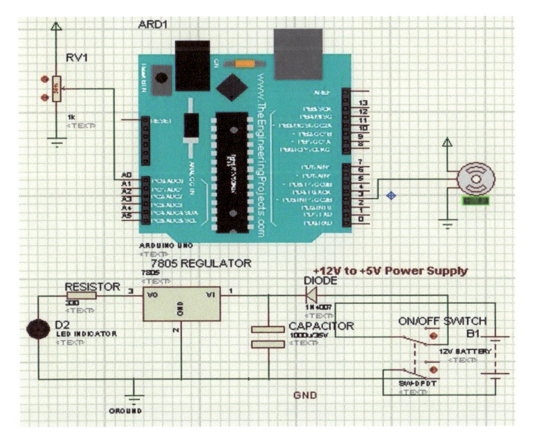

Fig. (6.3). Circuit diagram of the system.

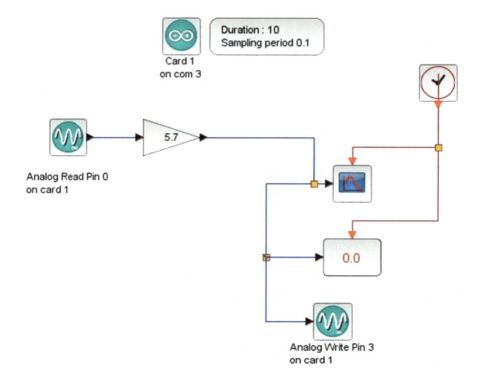

Fig. (6.4). XCOS Model for analog read/write.

CHAPTER 7

Motion Detection System with Arduino_1.1 Package

Abstract: This chapter discusses the working of a home automation system where lights of the room are made 'ON' if a human presence is detected, with the help of Scilab XCOS and Arduino I/O package. To understand the read/write operation with Scilab XCOS, a system is designed to automate a room where lights will be 'ON', if human presence is detected. Fig. (**7.1**) shows the block diagram of the system. The block diagram comprises of power supply, Arduino Nano, motion detector sensor (PIR), relay and Bulb.

Keywords: Arduino_1.1 Package, PIR sensor, Scilab.

The objective of the system is to read the PIR (Passive Infrared) sensor connected to digital pin and make bulb 'ON/OFF' w.r.t change in status of sensor, using Scilab XCOS and serial link (Arduino I/O package). Fig. (**7.1**) shows the block diagram of the system. The block diagram comprises of power supply, Arduino Nano, AC bulb and motion sensor (PIR). The chapter discusses the motion sensor as digital sensor which sends the status through serial link to Scilab XCOS and Arduino to make change in the status of bulb.

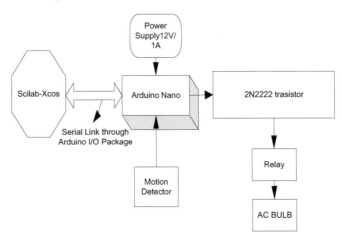

Fig. (7.1). Block diagram of the system.

Rajesh Singh, Anita Gehlot & Bhupendra Singh

Table **7.1** describes the components list, required to develop the system.

Table 7.1. Component list.

Components/ Device	Quality
Power Supply 12V/500mA	1
+12V to 5V converter	1
Power supply patch/ breakout	1
Arduino Nano	1
AC bulb	1
PIR sensor	1
M-F connector jumper wire	20
F-F connector jumper wire	20
M-M connector jumper wire	20
PC/Laptop with Scilab XCOS	1
Transistor 2N2222	1
AC Plug	1
Ice cube relay	1

Note: All components are available at www.nuttyengineer.com

PIR Motion Sensor

The Passive Infrared (PIR) sensor or Pyroelectric Infrared (PIR) sensor is a digital sensor, which is designed to detect the motion. It operates on 5V to 9V DC and requires 10-60 seconds of settling time before starting the operation. It comprises a fresnel lens and a motion detection circuit. By measuring the change in infrared levels, it can detect the motion within the range of 6 meters. Fig. (**7.2**) shows the PIR motion sensor. To control AC appliances relay board, there is a need to interface between controller and appliance. Fig. (**7.3**) shows relay board.

Fig. (7.2). PIR motion sensor.

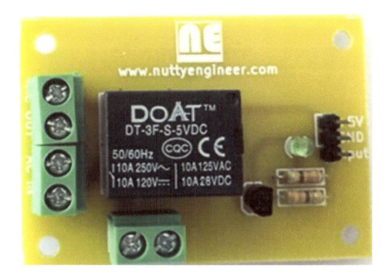

Fig. (7.3). Relay board.

7.1. CIRCUIT DIAGRAM

Fig. (**7.4**) shows the circuit diagram of the system. The circuit shows the interfacing connection of the PIR sensor, relay board, Arduino Nano and power supply.

The connections are as follows-

1. +12V and GND (ground) pin of power adaptor is connected with female DC jack of the Arduino Nano respectively.
2. +Vcc, GND, OUT pins of PIR sensor are connected to +5V, GND, D7 pins of Arduino Nano respectively.
3. Connect D6 pin to the base of transistor 2N2222, emitter of transistor is made ground, the collector is connected to 'L1' of relay, L2 is connected to +12V power supply.
4. Common terminal of relay is connected to one terminal of AC power source.
5. Second terminal of AC source is connected to one terminal of bulb.
6. 'NC' of relay is connected to second terminal of bulb.
7. Add the basic blocks to SCilab XCOS, as per requirement, as shown in Figs. (**7.5**) & (**7.6**).
8. Load the package to Arduino and check the working of the system.

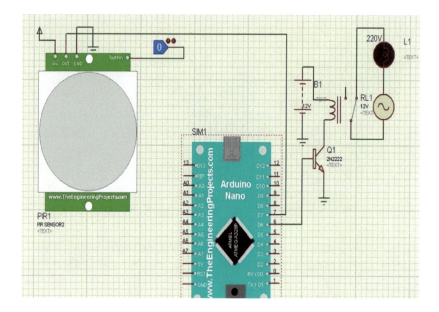

Fig. (7.4). Circuit diagram of the system.

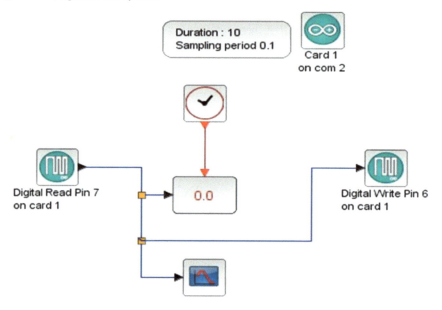

Fig. (7.5). XCOS Model for the system.

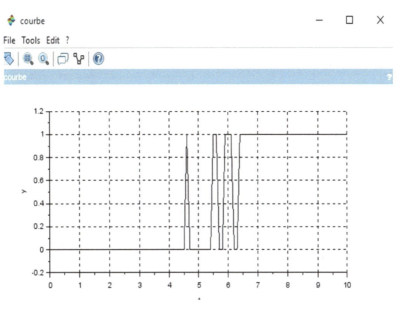

Fig. (7.6). XCOS Model waveform.

CHAPTER 8

Two Axis Solar Tracker with Arduino_1.1 Package

Abstract: This chapter discusses the working of two axis solar trekking system with the help of four LDRs and two servo motors. The control of system is described with the help of Scilab XCOS and Arduino I/O package. A two axis solar tracker is a system which can move in the two degree of freedom and the motion of axis is controlled w.r.t change in light intensity sensed by LDR.

Keywords: Arduino_1.1 package, LDR, Solar traker, Servo motor, Scilab.

The tracker moves to the direction where maximum light intensity is detected. Fig. (**8.1**) shows the block diagram of the system. The block diagram comprises power supply, Arduino Nano, LDR (Light dependent Resistor) sensor and servo motor. The objective of the system is to design a two axis solar tracker, using Scilab XCOS and serial link (Arduino I/O package). The position of the sun tracker can be changed by taking the decision from cumulative reading of analog LDR sensors.

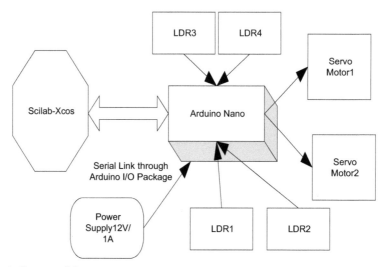

Fig. (8.1). Block diagram of the system.

Rajesh Singh, Anita Gehlot & Bhupendra Singh

Table **8.1** describes the components list, required to develop the system.

Table 8.1. Component list.

Components/ Device	Quality
Power Supply 12V/500mA	1
+12V to 5V converter	1
Power supply patch/ breakout	1
Arduino Nano	1
LDR	4
Servo motor	2
M-F connector jumper wire	20
F-F connector jumper wire	20
M-M connector jumper wire	20
PC/Laptop with Scilab XCOS	1

Note: All components are available at www.nuttyengineer.com

Servo Motor

A servomotor is an actuator, which may have rotary or linear motion. It allows precise control of angular or linear position, velocity and acceleration. It has a motor coupled with a sensor for position feedback. Fig. (**8.2**) shows the view of servo sensor.

Fig. (8.2). Servo motor.

8.1. CIRCUIT DIAGRAM

Fig. (**8.3**) shows the circuit diagram of the system. The circuit shows the interfacing connection of the LDR sensor, Arduino Nano, Servos and power supply.

The connections are as follows-

1. +12V and GND (ground) pin of power adaptor is connected with female DC jack of the Arduino Nano respectively.
2. +Vcc, GND, OUT pins of LDR1 sensor is connected to +5V, GND, A0 pin (analog read pin 0) of Arduino Nano respectively.
3. +Vcc, GND, OUT pins of LDR2 sensor is connected to +5V, GND, A1 pin (analog read pin 1) of Arduino Nano respectively.
4. +Vcc, GND, OUT pins of LDR3 sensor is connected to +5V, GND, A2 pin ((analog read pin 2) of Arduino Nano respectively.
5. +Vcc, GND, OUT pins of LDR4 sensor is connected to +5V, GND, A3 pin (analog read pin 3) of Arduino Nano respectively.
6. Connect +Vcc, GND and OUT pin of servo1 motor to pin 9 of Arduino Nano.
7. Connect +Vcc, GND and OUT pin of servo2 motor to pin 10 of Arduino Nano.
8. Add the basic blocks to Scilab XCOS, as per requirement, as shown in Fig. (**8.4**).
9. Load the package to Arduino and check the working of the system.

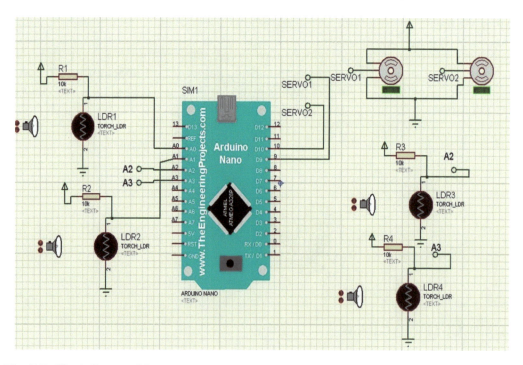

Fig. (8.3). Circuit diagram of the system.

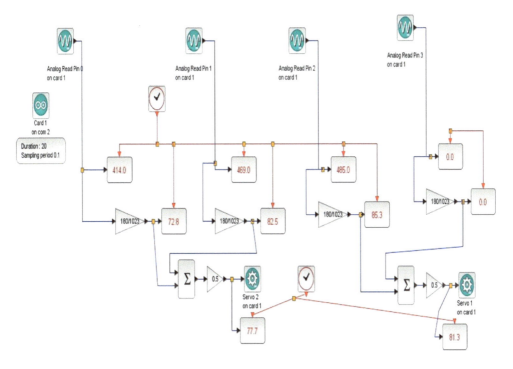

Fig. (8.4). XCOS Model for the system.

CHAPTER 9

Environment Parameter Monitoring System with Arduino_1.1 Package

Abstract: This chapter discusses the working of environment parameter monitoring system with analog and digital sensor interfacing. The control of system is described with the help of Scilab XCOS and Arduino I/O package. The section describes the method to read analog sensor and digital sensor like MQ3 sensor, MQ6 sensor, LM35 sensor, LDR sensor, Proximity sensor and IR sensor.

Keywords: Arduino_1.1 package, LDR, LM35, MQ3, MQ6, Scilab.

The section describes the method to read analog sensor and digital sensor like MQ3 sensor, MQ6 sensor, LM35 sensor, LDR sensor, proximity sensor and IR sensor as the parameters of environmental monitoring, using Arduino I/O package and Scilab XCOS model. Fig. (**9.1**) shows the block diagram of the system. The block diagram comprises Arduino Nano, MQ3 sensor, MQ6 sensor, LM35 sensor, LDR sensor, Proximity sensor, IR sensor and power supply 12V/1A with +12V to +5 V convertor. The objective of the chapter is to read the analog and digital sensors and communicate the sensory data to Scilab GUI.

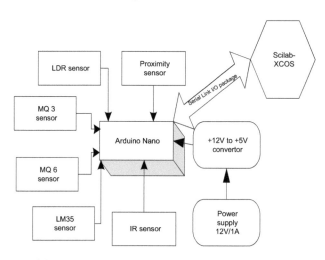

Fig. (9.1). Block diagram of the system.

Rajesh Singh, Anita Gehlot & Bhupendra Singh

Table **9.1** describes the components list, required to develop the system.

Table 9.1. Component List.

Components/ Device	Quality
Power Supply 12V/500mA	1
+12V to 5V converter	1
Power supply patch/ breakout	1
Arduino Nano	1
LDR	1
IR sensor	1
Proximity sensor	1
LM35	1
MQ3	1
MQ6	1
M-F connector jumper wire	20
F-F connector jumper wire	20
M-M connector jumper wire	20
PC/Laptop with Scilab XCOS	1

Note: All components are available at www.nuttyengineer.com

IR Sensor

IR (Infra Red) sensor is generally used for collision detection. The module comprises an IR emitter and IR receiver pair, potentiometer and comparator IC-358. Transmitter (Tx) and Receiver (Rx) are placed parallel to each other, as shown in Fig. (**9.2**) IR transmitter emits the light. When any obstacle comes in the path, it reflects back and the obstacle is detected.

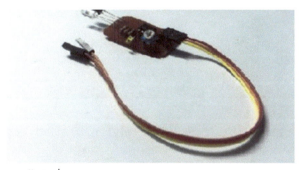

Fig. (9.2). IR sensor from nuttyengineer.com.

Gas Sensor

It can be used for detecting gas leakage (LPG, iso-butane, propane, LNG combustible gases), with detection range of 100 to 10000 PPM. It operates on 5V. The sensor has inbuilt heater which heats the sensing element. Fig. (**9.3**) shows the view of GAS sensor MQ6. It has warm up time of 10 min. To convert analog voltage into PPM follow the equation- PPM = (Analog Voltage in mV) x 2

Fig. (9.3). MQ6 from nuttyengineer.com.

The Proximity & Touch Sensor

It is a digital sensor. It works on the principle of change in the capacitance. The sensor has two types of output. The first output is called proximity output, which gives output when the finger is around 2cm above pad. Another output is touch output, which gets activated when the finger is just on the pad around 1mm above. Fig. (**9.4**) shows the proximity sensor.

Fig. (9.4). Proximity sensor from nuttyengineer.com.

LM35

LM35 is a temperature sensor, the output voltage of which is proportional to the Celsius (Centigrade) temperature. Its operating range is -55 to 150 °C. Fig. (**9.5**) shows the view of LM35 sensor.

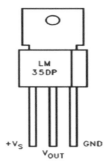

Fig. (9.5). Temperature sensor (LM35).

9.1. CIRCUIT DIAGRAM

Fig. (**9.6**) shows the circuit diagram of the system. The circuit shows the interfacing connection of MQ3 sensor, MQ6 sensor, LM35 sensor, LDR sensor, Proximity sensor and IR sensor, Arduino Nano, Servos and power supply.

The connections are as follows-

1. +12V and GND (ground) pin of power adaptor are connected with female DC jack of the Arduino Nano respectively.
2. +Vcc, GND, OUT pins of MQ3 sensor are connected to +5V, GND, A1 pin (analog read pin 1) of Arduino Nano respectively.
3. +Vcc, GND, OUT pins of MQ6 sensor are connected to +5V, GND, A2 pin (analog read pin 2) of Arduino Nano respectively.
4. +Vcc, GND, OUT pins of LDR sensor are connected to +5V, GND, A0 pin (analog read pin 0) of Arduino Nano respectively.
5. +Vcc, GND, OUT pins of touch proximity sensor are connected to +5V, GND, A3 pin (analog read pin 3) of Arduino Nano respectively.
6. +Vcc, GND, OUT pins of IR sensor are connected to +5V, GND, D7 pin of Arduino Nano respectively.
7. +Vcc, GND, OUT pins of LM35 sensor are connected to +5V, GND, D6 pin of Arduino Nano respectively.
8. Anode of LED1 is connected to D5 pin of Arduino Nano through resistor and cathode to GND (Ground).
9. Anode of LED2 is connected to D4 pin of Arduino Nano through resistor and cathode to GND (Ground).
10. Add the basic blocks to Scilab XCOS, as per requirement, as shown in Fig. (**9.7**).
11. Load the package to Arduino and check the working of the system.

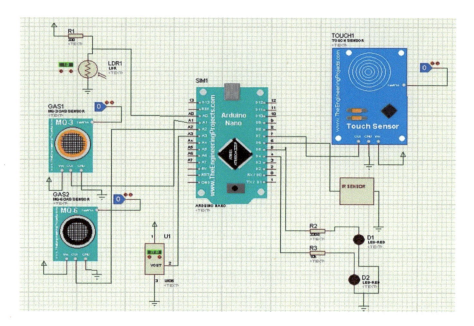

Fig. (9.6). Circuit diagram of the system.

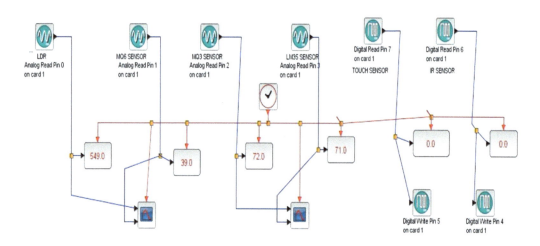

Fig. (9.7). XCOS model for the system.

Figs. (**9.8** and **9.9**) shows the waveform from sensory data.

Note- To get the temperature value divide voltage level by 2. *e.g* here 72/2=36.

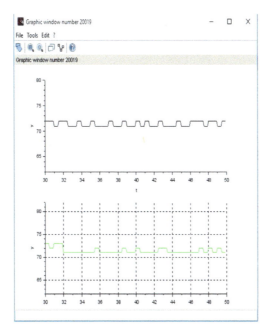

Fig. (9.8). Waveform1 is output (as voltage level) of MQ3 sensor and waveform2 from LM35 sensor.

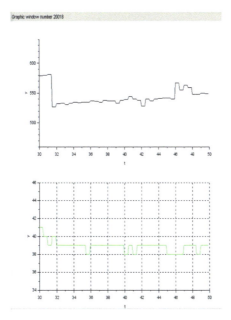

Fig. (9.9). Waveform1 is output (as voltage level) of LDR sensor and waveform2 from MQ6 sensor.

CHAPTER 10

Environment Parameter Monitoring Robot with Arduino_1.1 Package

Abstract: This chapter discusses the working of environment parameter monitoring robot along with analog and digital sensor interfacing. The control of robot is described with the help of Scilab XCOS and Arduino I/O package. The section describes the method to read analog sensor and digital sensor like MQ3 sensor, LM35 sensor, LDR sensor with the help of a robot.

Keywords: Arduino_1.1 package, LDR, LM35, MQ3, MQ6, Robot, Scilab.

The section describes the working of a robot along with the method to read analog sensor and digital sensor like MQ3 sensor, MQ6 sensor, LM35 sensor, LDR sensor, Proximity sensor and IR sensor as the parameters of environmental monitoring, using Arduino I/O package and Scilab XCOS model. Fig. (**10.1**) shows the block diagram of the system. The objective of the chapter is to design a robot which can collect the environment parameters from the surroundings.

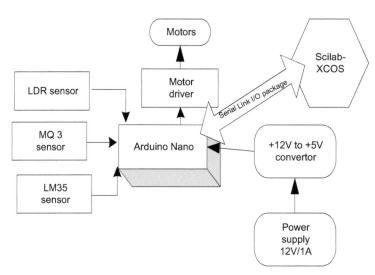

Fig. (10.1). Block diagram of the system.

Rajesh Singh, Anita Gehlot & Bhupendra Singh

Table **10.1** describes the components list, required to develop the system.

Table 10.1. Component list.

Components/ Device	Quality
Power Supply 12V/500mA	1
+12V to 5V converter	1
Power supply patch/ breakout	1
Arduino Nano	1
LDR	1
DC Motor	2
Motor driver (L293D)	1
LM35	1
MQ3	1
MQ6	1
M-F connector jumper wire	20
F-F connector jumper wire	20
M-M connector jumper wire	20
PC/Laptop with Scilab XCOS	1

Note: All components are available at www.nuttyengineer.com

10.1. CIRCUIT DIAGRAM

Fig. (**10.2**) shows the circuit diagram of the system. The circuit shows the interfacing connection of MQ3 sensor, LM35 sensor, LDR sensor, Motors, Motor driver, Arduino Nano, Servos and power supply.

The connections are as follows-

1. +12V and GND (ground) pin of power adaptor is connected with female DC jack of the Arduino Nano respectively.
2. +Vcc, GND, OUT pins of MQ3 is connected to +5V, GND, A0 pin (analog read pin 0) of Arduino Nano respectively.
3. +Vcc, GND, OUT pins of LM35 sensor is connected to +5V, GND, A1 pin (analog read pin 1) of Arduino Nano respectively.
4. +Vcc, GND, OUT pins of LDR sensor is connected to +5V, GND, A0 pin (analog read pin 0) of Arduino Nano respectively.
5. Connect 4, 5, 12 and 13 pins of L293D to the ground or GND of power supply.

6. Connect 2, 9 and 16 pins of L293D to the +Vcc or +5V of power supply.
7. Connect input pins 2, 7, 10 and 15 of L293D to the D7, D6, D5 and D4 pins of Arduino Nano respectively.
8. Connect output 3, 6, 11 and 14 of L293D to the + positive (red wire) and –negative (black wire) of first motor and + positive (red wire) and –negative (black wire) of second motor.
9. Add the basic blocks to Scilab XCOS, as per requirement, as shown in Fig. (**10.3**).
10. Load the package to Arduino and check the working of the system.

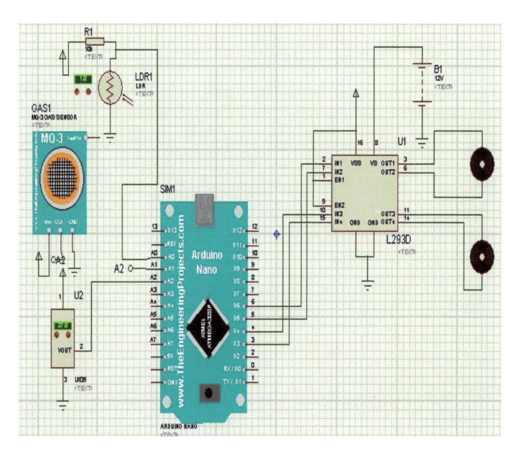

Fig. (10.2). Circuit diagram of the system.

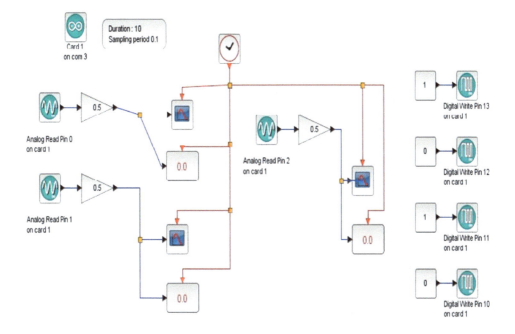

Fig. (10.3). Scilab XCOS model of the system.

CHAPTER 11

PID Controller for Heater with Arduino_1.1 Package

Abstract: This chapter explains the concept of PID and system to control the room temperature with the interfacing of temperature sensor and heater. The control of the system is described with the help of Scilab XCOS and Arduino I/O package.

Keywords: Arduino_1.1 Package, PID, Scilab.

PID stands for Proportional, Integral, and Derivative. It is a standard control structure used for many industrial applications. The system is set up after some setup and tuning the PID parameters.

The transfer function of PID controller is as follows-

$$C(s) = K_p + \frac{K_i}{s} + K_d s$$

Where

K_p – Proportional constant

K_i- Integral constant

K_d- Derivative constant

The weighted sum of three constants is used to adjust the process through a control element. The basic block diagram of conventional feedback control system, shown in Fig. (**11.1**).

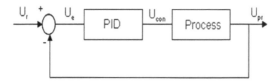

Fig. (11.1). PID block diagram.

To understand the working of PID controller, a system is discussed in this section. To control the room temperature, a threshold value of temperature needs to be set. The real time temperature value is measured with temperature sensor, connected to pin A0 of Arduino. The error signal is generated by calculating the difference between the set temperature value and feedback signal received from temperature sensor. This error signal is communicated to PID controller in XCOS and accordingly, the output signal is generated to achieve threshold value of temperature. Fig. (**11.2**) shows the block diagram of the system. The system comprises +12V power supply, +12V to +5V converter, Arduino Uno, LM 35 sensor, solid-state relay and heater element.

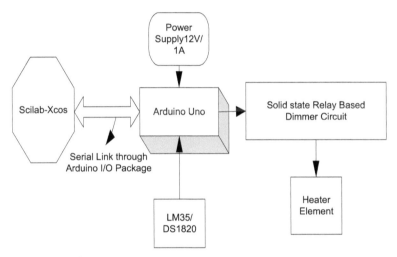

Fig. (11.2). Block diagram of the system.

Table **11.1** describes the components list, required to develop the system.

Table 11.1. Component list.

Components/ Device	Quality
Power Supply 12V/500mA	1
+12V to 5V converter	1
Power supply patch/ breakout	1
Arduino Uno	1
Temperature sensor	1
Relay	2
Heater element	1
M-F connector jumper wire	20

(Table 11.1) cont.....

Components/ Device	Quality
F-F connector jumper wire	20
M-M connector jumper wire	20
PC/Laptop with Scilab XCOS	1

Note: All components are available at www.nuttyengineer.com

11.1. CIRCUIT DIAGRAM

Fig. (**11.3**) shows the circuit diagram of the system. The circuit shows the interfacing connection of MQ3 sensor, LM35 sensor, LDR sensor, Arduino Uno, heater element and power supply.

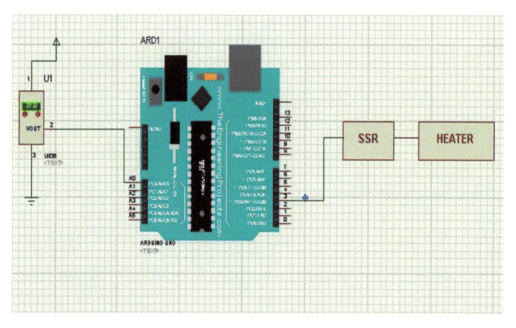

Fig. (11.3). Circuit Diagram of the system.

The connections are as follows-

1. +12V and GND (ground) pin of power adaptor is connected with female DC jack of the Arduino Uno respectively.
2. +Vcc, GND, OUT pins of LM35 sensor is connected to +5V, GND, A0 pins of Arduino Uno respectively.
3. Connect +Vcc, GND and IN pin of SSR (solid state relay) as dimmer to pin 3 of Arduino Uno to control the heater.

4. Add the basic blocks to Scilab XCOS, as per requirement, as shown in Fig. **(11.4)**.
5. Load the package to Arduino and check the working of the system.

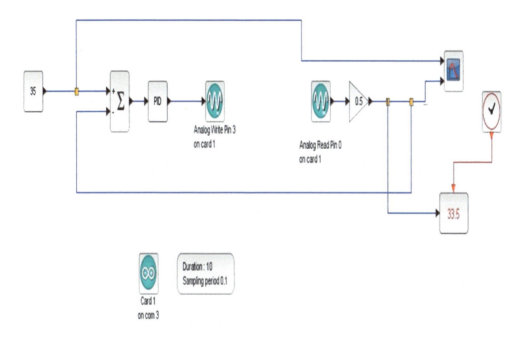

Fig. (11.4). XCOS model for the system.

CHAPTER 12

Wireless Building Automation System

Abstract: This chapter describes the wireless building automation system using Scilab without Arduino_1.1 package. Graphical user interface of Scilab controls the transmitter of the remote and receiver section takes the command to control the appliances of building.

Keywords: RF Modem, Scilab.

Wireless building automation system has two parts- transmitter section and receiver section. The transmitter is connected to Scilab and the receiver section is connected with 4-channel relay board to control the appliances. The transmitter section comprises Arduino Nano, RF modem, liquid crystal display (LCD), and power supply 12V/1A. The receiver section comprises of Arduino Nano, RF modem, liquid crystal display (LCD), 4 channel relay board, and power supply 12V/1A. Graphical user interface sends the command serially to the Arduino Nano board. The board receives the signal, displays the required data on liquid crystal display, and again send the data on serial port *via* wireless communication using RF modem. Fig. (**12.1**) shows the block diagram of transmitter section.

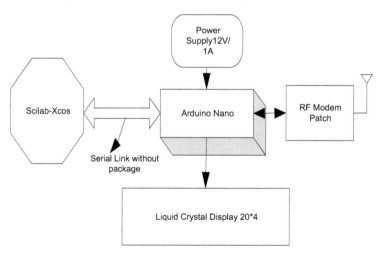

Fig. (12.1). Block diagram of transmitter section.

Rajesh Singh, Anita Gehlot & Bhupendra Singh

Table **12.1** describes the components list, required to develop the transmitter section.

Table 12.1. Component list for transmitter section.

Components/ Device	Quality
Power Supply 12V/500mA	1
+12V to 5V converter	1
Power supply patch/ breakout	1
Arduino Nano	1
LCD	1
LCD patch	1
RF modem	1
RF modem patch	1
M-F connector jumper wire	20
F-F connector jumper wire	20
M-M connector jumper wire	20
PC/Laptop with Scilab XCOS	1

Note: All components are available at www.nuttyengineer.com

Fig. (**12.2**) shows the receiver section. The receiver section receives the data command from the transmitter and makes four appliances (bulb, fan, exhaust fan, geyser) 'ON/OFF' through 4-channel relay board. The data commands are also displayed on liquid crystal display.

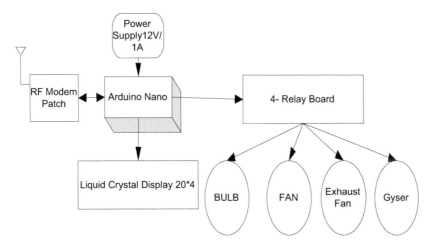

Fig. (12.2). Block diagram of receiver section.

Table **12.2** describes the components list, required to develop the receiver section.

Table 12.2. Component list for receiver section.

Components/ Device	Quality
Power Supply 12V/500mA	1
+12V to 5V converter	1
Power supply patch/ breakout	1
Arduino Nano	1
LCD	1
LCD patch	1
RF modem	1
RF modem patch	1
Four relay board	1
Home appliances	4
M-F connector jumper wire	20
F-F connector jumper wire	20
M-M connector jumper wire	20
PC/Laptop with Scilab XCOS	1

Note: All components are available at www.nuttyengineer.com

12.1. CIRCUIT DIAGRAM

The sections 12.1.1 describes the connections of transmitter section and section 12.1.2 describes the connections of receiver section. Figs. (**12.3**, **12.4** and **12.5**) show the circuit diagram of the transmitter and receiver with different appliance status.

12.1.1. Connections of Transmitter Section

1. +12V and GND (ground) pin of power adaptor is connected with female DC jack of the Arduino Nano respectively.
2. The +5V and GND (ground) pin of the power supply is connected to +5V and GND pin of LCD patch/ breakout board respectively.
3. Connect RS, RW and E pins of LCD to D12, GND and D11 of the Arduino Nano.
4. Connect D4, D5, D6 and D7 pins of LCD to D10, D9, D8 and D7 of the Arduino Nano.
5. +Vcc, GND, RX and TX pins of RF modem is connected to +5V, GND, TX and RX pins of Arduino Nano respectively.

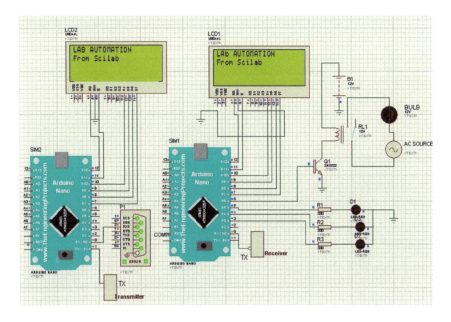

Fig. (12.3). Circuit diagram of the system.

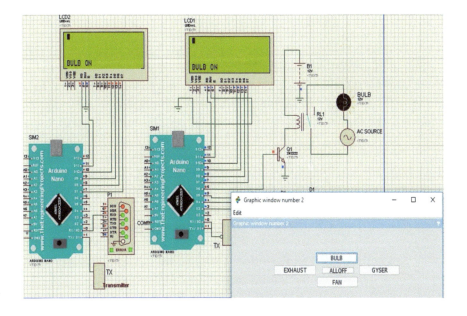

Fig. (12.4). Circuit showing bulb 'ON'.

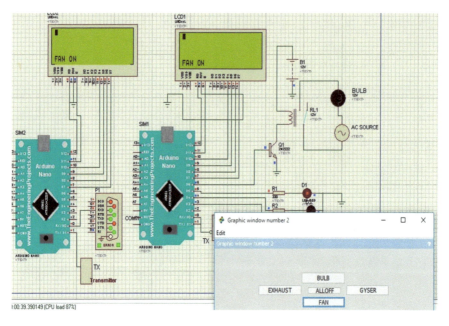

Fig. (12.5). Circuit showing Fan 'ON'.

12.1.2. Connections of Receiver Section

1. +12V and GND (ground) pin of power adaptor is connected with female DC jack of the Arduino Nano respectively.
2. The +5V and GND (ground) pin of the power supply is connected to +5V and GND pin of LCD patch/ breakout board respectively.
3. Connect RS, RW and E pins of LCD to D12, GND and D11 of the Arduino Nano.
4. Connect D4, D5, D6 and D7 pins of LCD to D10, D9, D8 and D7 of the Arduino Nano.
5. +Vcc, GND, RX and TX pins of RF modem is connected to +5V, GND, TX and RX pins of Arduino Nano respectively.
6. Connect relay1 input to pin6 of Arduino Nano and other terminal to the Ground (GND).
7. Connect load between 'NO' and 'COM' with 220V/50Hz AC voltage of relay1.
8. Connect relay2 input to pin5 of Arduino Nano and other terminal to the Ground (GND).
9. Connect load between 'NO' and 'COM' with 220V/50Hz AC voltage of relay2.
10. Connect relay3 input to pin4 of Arduino Nano and other terminal to the

Ground (GND).
11. Connect load between 'NO' and 'COM' with 220V/50Hz AC voltage of relay3.
12. Connect relay4 input to pin3 of Arduino Nano and other terminal to the Ground (GND).
13. Connect load between 'NO' and 'COM' with 220V/50Hz AC voltage of relay4.

12.2. PROGRAM CODE

The sections 12.2.1 shows the program code for transmitter section and section 12.2.2 shows the program code for receiver section of the system. Write these programs in Arduino IDE and burn into Arduino and check the working of the system.

12.2.1. Program Code for Transmitter Section

```
#include <LiquidCrystal.h> // add LCD library

LiquidCrystal lcd(12, 11, 10, 9, 8, 7); // pins of LCD connected to NodeMCU

void setup()

{

lcd.begin(20,4); // initialize the LCD

Serial.begin(9600); // initialize serial communication

lcd.setCursor(0,0); // set cursor on LCD

lcd.print("LAB AUTOMATION"); // print string on LCD

lcd.setCursor(0,1); // set cursor on LCD

lcd.print("From Scilab"); //print string on LCD

delay(1000); // provide delay of 1000 mSec

lcd.clear(); // clear the contents of LCD

}

void loop()

{
```

```
char SCILAB_SERIAL_CHAR;

SCILAB _SERIAL_CHAR=Serial.read(); // record serial data on defined
character

lcd.setCursor(0,0); // set cursor on LCD

lcd.print(SCILAB _SERIAL_CHAR); // print the value on the LCD

if (SCILAB _SERIAL_CHAR=='a') // // check char for Scilab

{

lcd.clear(); // clear the contents of the LCD

lcd.setCursor(0,3); // set cursor on LCD

lcd.print("BULB ON"); // print string on LCD

Serial.write(10); // serial write the value 10 on serial port

}

else if (SCILAB _SERIAL_CHAR=='b') // check char for Scilab

{

lcd.clear(); // clear the contents of the LCD

lcd.setCursor(0,3); // set cursor on LCD

lcd.print("FAN ON"); //print string on LCD

Serial.write(20); // serial write the value 20 on serial port

}

else if (SCILAB _SERIAL_CHAR=='c') // check char for Scilab

{

lcd.clear(); //clear the contents of the LCD

lcd.setCursor(0,3); // set cursor on LCD

lcd.print("EXHAUST ON"); // print string on LCD
```

```
Serial.write(30); // serial write the value 30 on serial port

}

else if (SCILAB _SERIAL_CHAR=='d') // check char for Scilab

{

lcd.clear(); // clear the contents of the LCD

lcd.setCursor(0,3); // set cursor on LCD

lcd.print("GYSER ON"); // print string on LCD

Serial.write('d'); // print string on LCD

}

else if (SCILAB _SERIAL_CHAR=='e') // check char for Scilab

{

lcd.clear(); // clear the contents of the LCD

lcd.setCursor(0,3); // set cursor on LCD

lcd.print("ALL OFF"); // print string on LCD

Serial.write(50); // print string on LCD

}

delay(10); // provide the delay

}
```

12.2.2. Program Code for Receiver Section

```
#include <LiquidCrystal.h> // add library

LiquidCrystal lcd(12, 11, 10, 9, 8, 7); // LCD pins connected to Arduino Nano

int BULB=6; // assign pin 6 for relay for BULB

int FAN=5; // assign pin 6 for relay for FAN

int EXHAUST_FAN=4; // assign pin 6 for relay for FAN
```

```
int GYSER=3; // assign pin 6 for relay for GYSER

void setup()

{

lcd.begin(20,4); // Initialize LCD

Serial.begin(9600); // Initialize serial

lcd.setCursor(0,0); // set cursor on LCD

lcd.print("Lab AUTOMATION"); // print string on LCD

lcd.setCursor(0,1); // set cursor on LCD

lcd.print("From Scilab"); // print string on LCD

pinMode(BULB,OUTPUT); // set bulb as output

pinMode(FAN,OUTPUT); // set fan as output

pinMode(EXHAUST_FAN,OUTPUT); // set exhaust fan as output

pinMode(GYSER,OUTPUT); // set Gyser as output

delay(1000); // provide delay of 1000 mSec

lcd.clear(); // clear the LCD

}

void loop()

{

char SCILAB _SERIAL_CHAR;

SCILAB _SERIAL_CHAR=Serial.read(); // record serial data

lcd.setCursor(0,0); // set cursor on LCD

lcd.print (SCILAB _SERIAL_CHAR); // print value on serial

if (SCILAB _SERIAL_CHAR==10) // check value

{
```

```
lcd.clear(); // clear LCD

lcd.setCursor(0,3); // set cursor on LCD

lcd.print("BULB ON"); // print string of LCD

digitalWrite(BULB,HIGH); // make BULB pin HIGH

digitalWrite(FAN,LOW); // make FAN pin LOW

digitalWrite(EXHAUST_FAN,LOW); ///// make exhaust fan pin LOW

digitalWrite(GYSER,LOW); // // make GYSER pin LOW

}

else if (SCILAB _SERIAL_CHAR==20)

{

lcd.clear(); // clear LCD

lcd.setCursor(0,3); // set cursor on LCD

lcd.print("FAN ON"); // print string of LCD

digitalWrite(BULB,LOW); // make BULB pin LOW

digitalWrite(FAN,HIGH); // make FAN pin HIGH

digitalWrite(EXHAUST_FAN,LOW); // make exhaust fan pin LOW

digitalWrite(GYSER,LOW); // make Gyser pin LOW

}

else if (SCILAB _SERIAL_CHAR==30)

{

lcd.clear(); // clear LCD

lcd.setCursor(0,3); // set cursor on LCD

lcd.print("EXHAUST ON"); // print string on LCD

digitalWrite(BULB,LOW); // make BULB pin LOW
```

```
digitalWrite(FAN,LOW); // make FAN pin LOW

digitalWrite(EXHAUST_FAN,HIGH); // // make Exhaust fan pin HIGH

digitalWrite(GYSER,LOW); // // make Gyser pin LOW

}

else if (SCILAB _SERIAL_CHAR==40) // check value

{

lcd.clear(); // clear the contents of LCD

lcd.setCursor(0,3); // set cursor on LCD

lcd.print("GYSER ON"); // print string on LCD

digitalWrite(BULB,LOW); // make BULB pin LOW

digitalWrite(FAN,LOW); // // make FAN pin LOW

digitalWrite(EXHAUST_FAN,LOW); // make exhaust fan LOW

digitalWrite(GYSER,HIGH); // make Geyser pin HIGH

}

else if (SCILAB _SERIAL_CHAR==50) // check value

{

lcd.clear(); // clear the contents of LCD

lcd.setCursor(0,3); // set cursor on LCD

lcd.print("ALL OFF"); // print string on LCD

digitalWrite(BULB,LOW); // make BULB pin LOW

digitalWrite(FAN,LOW); // make FAN pin LOW

digitalWrite(EXHAUST_FAN,LOW); // make Exhaust pin LOW

digitalWrite(GYSER,LOW); // make Geyser pin LOW

}
```

}

12.3. GRAPHICAL USER INTERFACE IN SCILAB

Follow the steps to design the Scilab GUI, as discussed in chapter-4 and write the call back commands as follows-

1. Open the .sce file where following function will appear-

function BULB_callback (handles), function FAN_callback (handles), function EXAUST_callback (handles), function GEYSER_callback (handles) and function ALLOFF_callback(handles).

2. Inside these function write three commands -

function BULB_callback (handles)

h=openserial(1,"9600,n,8,1");

writeserial(h,"a");

closeserial(h);

endfunction

3. The overall program for the GUI is as follows-

// *This GUI file is generated by guibuilder version 3.0*

f=figure('figure_position',[400,50],'figure_size',[656,582],'auto_resize','on','backgr ound',[33],'figure_name','Graphic window number %d');

delmenu(f.figure_id,gettext('File'))

delmenu(f.figure_id,gettext('?'))

delmenu(f.figure_id,gettext('Tools'))

toolbar(f.figure_id,'off')

handles.dummy = 0;

handles.BULB=uicontrol(f,'unit','normalized','BackgroundColor',[-1,-1,1], 'Enable','on','FontAngle','normal','FontName','Tahoma','FontSize',[12],'FontUnits',' points','FontWeight','normal','ForegroundColor',[-1,-1,-1],'HorizontalAlignment', 'center','ListboxTop',[],'Max',[1],'Min',[0],'Position',[0.4072678,0.7487319,0.1859 375,0.1541667],'Relief','default','SliderStep',[0.01,0.1],'String','BULB','Style','push button','Value',[0],'VerticalAlignment','middle','Visible','on','Tag','BULB','Callbac k','BULB_callback(handles)')

handles.FAN=uicontrol(f,'unit','normalized','BackgroundColor',[-1,-1,-1], 'Enable','on','FontAngle','normal','FontName','Tahoma','FontSize',[12],'FontUnits',' points','FontWeight','normal','ForegroundColor',[-1,-1,-1],'HorizontalAlignment', 'center','ListboxTop',[],'Max',[1],'Min',[0],'Position',[0.3982353,0.3173246,0.1890 625,0.1541667],'Relief','default','SliderStep',[0.01,0.1],'String','FAN','Style','pushb utton','Value',[0],'VerticalAlignment','middle','Visible','on','Tag','FAN','Callback',' FAN_callback(handles)')

handles.EXHAUST=uicontrol(f,'unit','normalized','BackgroundColor',[-1,-1,-1], 'Enable','on','FontAngle','normal','FontName','Tahoma','FontSize',[12],'FontUnits',' points','FontWeight','normal','ForegroundColor',[-1,-1,-1],'HorizontalAlignment', 'center','ListboxTop',[],'Max',[1],'Min',[0],'Position',[0.1403279,0.5603080,0.1740 625,0.1304167],'Relief','default','SliderStep',[0.01,0.1],'String','EXHAUST','Style', 'pushbutton','Value',[0],'VerticalAlignment','middle','Visible','on','Tag','EXHAUS T','Callback',' EXHAUST _callback(handles)')

handles.GEYSER=uicontrol(f,'unit','normalized','BackgroundColor',[-1,-1,-1], 'Enable','on','FontAngle','normal','FontName','Tahoma','FontSize',[12],'FontUnits',' points','FontWeight','normal','ForegroundColor',[-1,-1,-1],'HorizontalAlignment', 'center','ListboxTop',[],'Max',[1],'Min',[0],'Position',[0.6810929,0.5580435,0.1634 375,0.1116667],'Relief','default','SliderStep',[0.01,0.1],'String','GEYSER','Style','p ushbutton','Value',[0],'VerticalAlignment','middle','Visible','on','Tag','GEYSER','C allback',' GEYSER _callback(handles)')

handles.ALLOFF=uicontrol(f,'unit','normalized','BackgroundColor',[-1,-1,-1], 'Enable','on','FontAngle','normal','FontName','Tahoma','FontSize',[12],'FontUnits',' points','FontWeight','normal','ForegroundColor',[-1,-1,-1],'HorizontalAlignment', 'center','ListboxTop',[],'Max',[1],'Min',[0],'Position',[0.4291257,0.5559239,0.1434 375,0.1029167],'Relief','default','SliderStep',[0.01,0.1],'String','ALLOFF','Style','p ushbutton','Value',[0],'VerticalAlignment','middle','Visible','on','Tag','ALLOFF','C allback',' ALLOFF_callback(handles)')

// Callbacks are defined as below. Please do not delete the comments as it will be used in coming version

function BULB_callback(**handles**)

//Write your callback for BULB here

//Write your callback for BULB here

h=openserial(1,"9600,n,8,1");

writeserial(h,"a");

closeserial(h);

endfunction

function FAN_callback(**handles**)

//Write your callback for FAN here

h=openserial(1,"9600,n,8,1");

writeserial(h,"b");

closeserial(h);

endfunction

function EXHAUST_callback(**handles**)

//Write your callback for EXHAUST here

h=openserial(1,"9600,n,8,1");

writeserial(h,"c");

closeserial(h);

endfunction

function GEYSER_callback(**handles**)

//Write your callback for GEYSER here

h=openserial(1,"9600,n,8,1");

writeserial(h,"d");

closeserial(h);

endfunction

function ALLOFF_callback(**handles**)

//Write your callback for ALLOFF here

h=openserial(1,"9600,n,8,1");

writeserial(h,"e");

closeserial(h);

endfunction

4. Run the .sce file and get the GUI, as shown in Fig. (**12.6**).

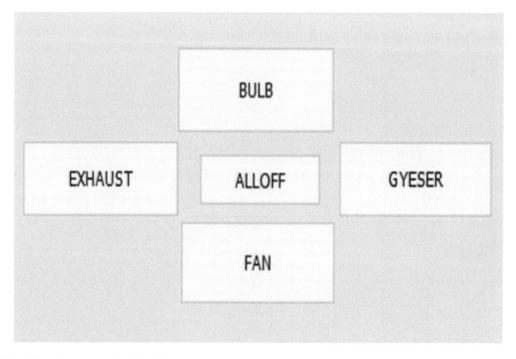

Fig. (12.6). Snapshot of Scilab GUI.

Arduino and SCILAB based Projects, 2019, 111-124

CHAPTER 13

Wireless Robot Control with Scilab GUI

Abstract: This chapter describes the wireless robot control using Scilab without Arduino_1.1 package. Graphical user interface of Scilab controls the transmitter of the remote and the receiver section takes the command to control the movement and direction of robot.

Keywords: GUI, Robot, Scilab.

Wireless robot control has two parts- transmitter section and receiver section. The transmitter is connected to Scilab and receiver section is connected with motor driver L293D to control the direction of the robot. The transmitter section comprises Arduino Nano, RF modem, liquid crystal display (LCD), and power supply 12V/1A. The receiver section/robot comprises Arduino Nano, RF modem, liquid crystal display (LCD), DC motors, motor driver, power supply 12V/1A. The graphical user interface sends the command serially to the Arduino Nano board. The board receives the signal, displays the required data on liquid crystal display, and again sends the data on serial port *via* wireless communication using RF modem. Fig. (**13.1**) shows the block diagram of transmitter section.

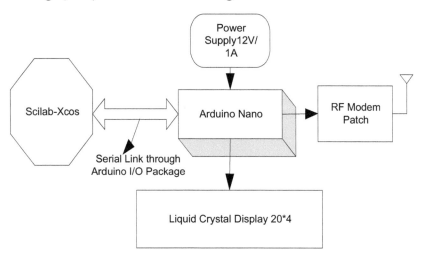

Fig. (13.1). Block diagram of transmitter section.

Rajesh Singh, Anita Gehlot & Bhupendra Singh

Table **13.1** describes the components list, required to develop the transmitter section.

Table 13.1. Component list for transmitter section.

Components/Device	Quality
Power Supply 12V/500mA	1
+12V to 5V converter	1
Power supply patch/ breakout	1
Arduino Nano	1
LCD	1
LCD patch	1
RF modem	1
RF modem patch	1
M-F connector jumper wire	20
F-F connector jumper wire	20
M-M connector jumper wire	20
PC/Laptop with Scilab XCOS	1

Note: All components are available at www.nuttyengineer.com

Fig. (**13.2**) shows the receiver section. The receiver section receives the data command from transmitter to make robot move 'Forward', 'Reverse', 'Right', 'Left' and 'Stop'. The data commands are also displayed on liquid crystal display.

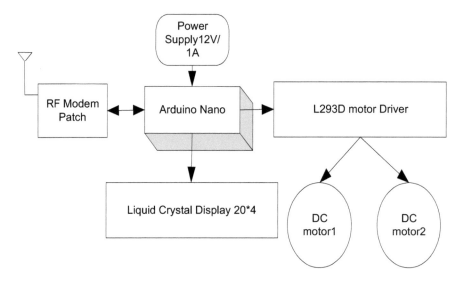

Fig. (13.2). Block diagram of receiver section.

Table **13.2** describes the components list, required to develop the receiver section.

Table 13.1. Component list for receiver section.

Components/ Device	Quality
Power Supply 12V/500mA	1
+12V to 5V converter	1
Power supply patch/ breakout	1
Arduino Nano	1
LCD	1
LCD patch	1
DC motors	2
Motor driver L293D	1
RF modem	1
RF modem patch	1
M-F connector jumper wire	20
F-F connector jumper wire	20
M-M connector jumper wire	20
PC/Laptop with Scilab XCOS	1

Note: All components are available at www.nuttyengineer.com

13.1. CIRCUIT DIAGRAM

Section 13.1.1 describes the connections of transmitter section and section 13.1.2 describes the connections of receiver section. Figs. (**13.3**,**13.4** and **13.5**) show the circuit diagram of the system with different movement of the robot.

13.1.1. Connections For Transmitter Section.

1. +12V and GND (ground) pin of power adaptor are connected with female DC jack of the Arduino Nano respectively.
2. +5V and GND (ground) pin of the power supply are connected to +5V and GND pin of LCD patch/ breakout board respectively.
3. Connect RS, RW and E pins of LCD to D12, GND and D11 of the Arduino Nano.
4. Connect D4, D5, D6 and D7 pins of LCD to D10, D9, D8 and D7 of the Arduino Nano.
5. +Vcc, GND, RX and TX pins of RF modem are connected to +5V, GND, TX and RX pins of Arduino Nano respectively.

13.1.2. Connections for Receiver Section.

1. +12V and GND (ground) pin of power adaptor is connected with female DC jack of the Arduino Nano respectively.
2. +5V and GND (ground) pin of the power supply is connected to +5V and GND pin of LCD patch/ breakout board respectively.
3. Connect RS, RW and E pins of LCD to D12, GND and D11 of the Arduino Nano.
4. Connect D4, D5, D6 and D7 pins of LCD to D10, D9, D8 and D7 of the Arduino Nano.
5. +Vcc, GND, RX and TX pins of RF modem are connected to +5V, GND, TX and RX pins of Arduino Nano respectively.
6. Connect 4, 5, 12 and 13 pins of L293D to the ground or GND of power supply.
7. Connect 2, 9 and 16 pins of L293D to the +Vcc or +5V of power supply.
8. Connect input pins 2, 7, 10 and 15 of L293D to the 7, 6, 5 and 4 pins of Arduino Nano respectively.
9. Connect output 3, 6, 11 and 14 of L293D to the + positive (red wire) and –negative (black wire) of first motor and + positive (red wire) and –negative (black wire) of second motor.

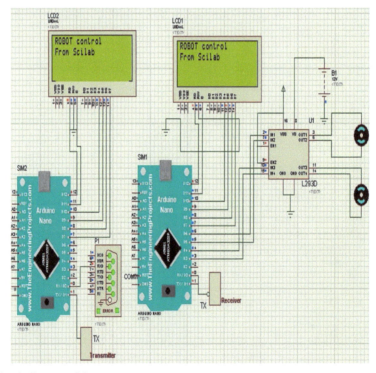

Fig. (13.3). Circuit diagram of the system.

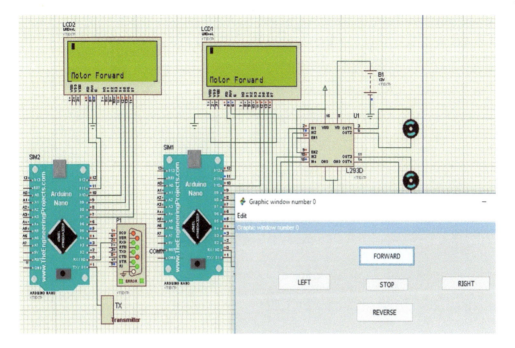

Fig. (13.4). Circuit showing the robot motion in 'Forward' direction.

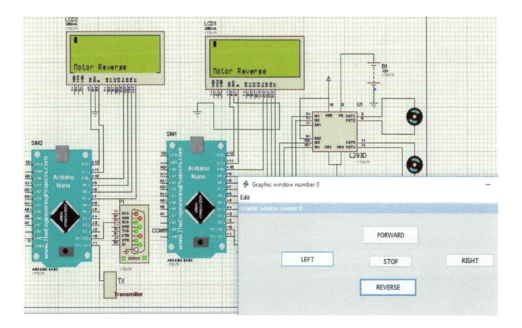

Fig. (13.5). Circuit showing the robot motion in 'Reverse' direction.

13.2. PROGRAM CODE

The section 13.2.1 shows the code for transmitter section and section 13.2.2 shows the program code for receiver section.

13.2.1. Program Code for Transmitter Section (Scilab Side)

```
#include <LiquidCrystal.h> // add library of LCD.

LiquidCrystal lcd(12, 11, 10, 9, 8, 7); // connect pins of LCD to the Arduino nano

void setup()

{

 lcd.begin(20,4); // initialize LCD

 Serial.begin(9600); // Initialize serial communication

 lcd.setCursor(0,0); // set cursor on LCD

 lcd.print("ROBOT control"); // print string on LCD

 lcd.setCursor(0,1); // set cursor on LCD

 lcd.print("From Scilab"); // print string on LCD

 delay(1000); // wait for 1000 mSec

 lcd.clear(); // clear LCD

}

void loop()

{

char SCILAB _SERIAL_CHAR;

SCILAB _SERIAL_CHAR=Serial.read(); // store data variable

  lcd.setCursor(0,0); // set cursor on LCD

  lcd.print(SCILAB _SERIAL_CHAR); // print variable on LCD

if (SCILAB _SERIAL_CHAR=='a') // check char on serial
```

```
{

  lcd.clear(); // clear LCD

  lcd.setCursor(0,3); // set cursor on LCD

  lcd.print("Motor Forward"); // print string on LCD

  Serial.write('a'); // send char to RF modem for Wireless communication

}
else if (SCILAB _SERIAL_CHAR=='b') // check char on serial

{

 lcd.clear(); // clear LCD

 lcd.setCursor(0,3); // set cursor on LCD

  lcd.print("Motor reverse"); // print string on LCD

  Serial.write('b'); // send char to RF modem for Wireless communication

}
 else if (SCILAB _SERIAL_CHAR=='c') // check char on serial

 {

 lcd.clear(); // clear LCD

 lcd.setCursor(0,3); // set cursor on LCD

 lcd.print("Motor Left"); // print string on LCD

  Serial.write('c'); //send char to RF modem for Wireless communication

}
else if (SCILAB _SERIAL_CHAR=='d') // check char on serial

{

 lcd.clear(); // clear LCD

lcd.setCursor(0,3); // set cursor on LCD
```

lcd.print("Motor Right"); // print string on LCD

Serial.write('d'); // send char to RF modem for Wireless communication

}

else if (SCILAB _SERIAL_CHAR=='e') // check char on serial

{

 lcd.clear(); // clear LCD

lcd.setCursor(0,3); // set cursor on LCD

lcd.print("STOP"); // print string on LCD

Serial.write('e'); // send char to RF modem for Wireless communication

}

delay(10); // wait for 10 mSec

}

13.2.2. Program Code for Receiver Section.

#include <LiquidCrystal.h> // add library of LCD

LiquidCrystal lcd(12, 11, 10, 9, 8, 7); // connect pins of LCD to Arduino Nano

int M1_POSITIVE=6; // connect +Positive pin of motor1 to pin 6 of Arduino Nano

int M1_NEGATIVE=5; // connect +negative pin of motor1 to pin 5 of Arduino Nano

int M2_POSITIVE=4; // connect +Positive pin of motor1 to pin 4 of Arduino Nano

int M2_NEGATIVE=3; // connect +Positive pin of motor1 to pin 3of Arduino Nano

void setup()

{

 lcd.begin(20,4); // initialize LCD

```
Serial.begin(9600); // Initialise serial communication

lcd.setCursor(0,0); // set cursor on LCD

lcd.print("ROBOT control"); // print string on LCD

lcd.setCursor(0,1); // set cursor on LCD

lcd.print("From Scilab"); // print string on LCD

 pinMode(M1_POSITIVE,OUTPUT); // set pin 6 to OUTPUT

  pinMode(M1_NEGATIVE,OUTPUT); // set pin 5 to OUTPUT

   pinMode(M2_POSITIVE,OUTPUT); // set pin 4 to OUTPUT

    pinMode(M2_NEGATIVE,OUTPUT); // set pin 3 to OUTPUT

 delay(1000); // wait for 1000 mSec

lcd.clear(); // clear LCD pin

}

void loop()

{

char SCILAB _SERIAL_CHAR;

SCILAB _SERIAL_CHAR=Serial.read(); // store serial coming data from
transmitter

lcd.setCursor(0,0); // set cursor on LCD

lcd.print(SCILAB _SERIAL_CHAR); // print value on LCD

 if (SCILAB _SERIAL_CHAR=='a') // check serial

 {

  lcd.clear(); // clear LCD

  lcd.setCursor(0,3); // set cursor on LCD

  lcd.print("Motor Forward"); // print string on LCD
```

```
  digitalWrite(M1_POSITIVE,HIGH); // set positive pin HIGH of motor1

  digitalWrite(M1_NEGATIVE,LOW); // set negative pin LOW of motor1

  digitalWrite(M2_POSITIVE,HIGH); // set positive pin HIGH of motor2

  digitalWrite(M2_NEGATIVE,LOW); // set negative pin LOW of motor2

}

else if (SCILAB _SERIAL_CHAR=='b') // check serial

{

  lcd.clear(); // clear LCD

  lcd.setCursor(0,3); // set cursor on LCD

  lcd.print("Motor Reverse"); // print string on LCD

  digitalWrite(M1_POSITIVE,LOW); // set positive pin LOW of motor1

  digitalWrite(M1_NEGATIVE,HIGH); // set negative pin HIGH of motor1

  digitalWrite(M2_POSITIVE,LOW); // set positive pin LOW of motor2

  digitalWrite(M2_NEGATIVE,HIGH); // // set negative pin HIGH of motor2

}

else if (SCILAB _SERIAL_CHAR=='c') // check serial

{

  lcd.clear(); // clear LCD

  lcd.setCursor(0,3); //set cursor on LCD

  lcd.print("Motor Left"); // print string on LCD

  digitalWrite(M1_POSITIVE,HIGH); //set positive pin HIGH of motor1

  digitalWrite(M1_NEGATIVE,LOW); // set negative pin LOW of motor1

  digitalWrite(M2_POSITIVE,LOW); // set positive pin LOW of motor2

  digitalWrite(M2_NEGATIVE,LOW); //// set negative pin LOW of motor2
```

```
}
else if (SCILAB _SERIAL_CHAR=='d') // check serial
{

    lcd.clear(); // clear LCD

    lcd.setCursor(0,3); // set cursor on LCD

    lcd.print("Motor Right"); // // print string on LCD

    digitalWrite(M1_POSITIVE,LOW); // set positive pin LOW of motor1

    digitalWrite(M1_NEGATIVE,LOW); // set negative pin LOW of motor1

    digitalWrite(M2_POSITIVE,HIGH); // set positive pin HIGH of motor2

    digitalWrite(M2_NEGATIVE,LOW); //set negative pin LOW of motor2

}
else if (SCILAB _SERIAL_CHAR=='e') // check serial
{

    lcd.clear(); // clear LCD

    lcd.setCursor(0,3); // set cursor on LCD

    lcd.print("STOP"); // print string on LCD

    digitalWrite(M1_POSITIVE,LOW); // set positive pin LOW of motor1

    digitalWrite(M1_NEGATIVE,LOW); //set negative pin LOW of motor1

    digitalWrite(M2_POSITIVE,LOW); // set positive pin LOW of motor2

    digitalWrite(M2_NEGATIVE,LOW); // set negative pin LOW of motor2

}
delay(10); // wait for 10mSec

}
```

13.3. GRAPHICAL USER INTERFACE IN SCILAB

Follow the steps to design the Scilab GUI, as discussed in chapter-4 and write the call back commands as follows-

1. Open the .sce file where following function will appear-
   function BULB_callback (handles), function FAN_callback (handles), function EXAUST_callback (handles), function GEYSER_callback (handles) and function ALLOFF_callback(handles).

2. Inside these function write three commands-
   function BULB_callback (handles)
    h=openserial(1,"9600,n,8,1");
   writeserial(h,"a");
   closeserial(h);
   endfunction

3. The overall program for the GUI is as follows-
   function FORWARD_callback (handles), function REVERSE_callback (handles), function LEFT_callback (handles), function RIGHT_callback (handles) and function STOP_callback(handles).
   Inside these function we have to write three commands inside it
   function FORWARD_callback (**handles**)
    h=openserial(1,"9600,n,8,1");
   writeserial(h,"a");
   closeserial(h);
   endfunction

4. The overall program for the GUI is given Below

   // This GUI file is generated by guibuilder version 3.0.
   f=figure('figure_position',[400,50],'figure_size',[656,582],'auto_resize','on','bac
   kground',[33],'figure_name','Graphic window number %d');
   delmenu(f.figure_id,gettext('File'))
   delmenu(f.figure_id,gettext('?'))
   delmenu(f.figure_id,gettext('Tools'))
   toolbar(f.figure_id,'off')
   handles.dummy = 0;
   handles.FORWARD=uicontrol(f,'unit','normalized','BackgroundColor',[-1,-1, -
   1],'Enable','on','FontAngle','normal','FontName','Tahoma','FontSize',[12], 'Font-
   Units','points','FontWeight','normal','ForegroundColor',[-1,-1,-1], 'Horizontal-
   Alignment','center','ListboxTop',[],'Max',[1],'Min',[0],'Position',[0.4072678,

0.7487319,0.1859375,0.1541667],'Relief','default','SliderStep',[0.01,0.1],'String
','FORWARD','Style','pushbutton','Value',[0],'VerticalAlignment','middle','Visi
ble','on','Tag','FORWARD','Callback','FORWARD_callback(handles)').
handles.REVERSE=uicontrol(f,'unit','normalized','BackgroundColor',[-1,-1,-1],
'Enable','on','FontAngle','normal','FontName','Tahoma','FontSize',[12],'FontUnit
s','points','FontWeight','normal','ForegroundColor',[-1,-1,-1], 'HorizontalAlignment','center','ListboxTop',[],'Max',[1],'Min',[0],'Position',[0.3982353,
0.3173246,0.1890625,0.1541667],'Relief','default','SliderStep',[0.01,0.1],'String
','REVERSE','Style','pushbutton','Value',[0],'VerticalAlignment','middle','Visibl
e','on','Tag','REVERSE','Callback','REVERSE_callback(handles)').
handles.LEFT=uicontrol(f,'unit','normalized','BackgroundColor',[-1,-1,-1],
'Enable','on','FontAngle','normal','FontName','Tahoma','FontSize',[12],'FontUnit
s','points','FontWeight','normal','ForegroundColor',[-1,-1,-1], 'HorizontalAlignment','center','ListboxTop',[],'Max',[1],'Min',[0],'Position',[0.1403279,
0.5603080,0.1740625,0.1304167],'Relief','default','SliderStep',[0.01,0.1],'String
','LEFT','Style','pushbutton','Value',[0],'VerticalAlignment','middle','Visible','on'
,'Tag','LEFT','Callback','LEFT_callback(handles)').
handles.RIGHT=uicontrol(f,'unit','normalized','BackgroundColor',[-1,-1,-1],
'Enable','on','FontAngle','normal','FontName','Tahoma','FontSize',[12],'FontUnit
s','points','FontWeight','normal','ForegroundColor',[-1,-1,-1], 'HorizontalAlignment','center','ListboxTop',[],'Max',[1],'Min',[0],'Position',[0.6810929,
0.5580435,0.1634375,0.1116667],'Relief','default','SliderStep',[0.01,0.1],'String
','RIGHT','Style','pushbutton','Value',[0],'VerticalAlignment','middle','Visible','o
n','Tag','RIGHT','Callback','RIGHT_callback(handles)').
handles.STOP=uicontrol(f,'unit','normalized','BackgroundColor',[-1,-1,-1],
'Enable','on','FontAngle','normal','FontName','Tahoma','FontSize',[12],'FontUnit
s','points','FontWeight','normal','ForegroundColor',[-1,-1,-1], 'HorizontalAlignment','center','ListboxTop',[],'Max',[1],'Min',[0],'Position',[0.4291257,
0.5559239,0.1434375,0.1029167],'Relief','default','SliderStep',[0.01,0.1],'String
','STOP','Style','pushbutton','Value',[0],'VerticalAlignment','middle','Visible','on'
,'Tag','STOP','Callback','STOP_callback(handles)').
// Callbacks are defined as below. Please do not delete the comments as it will
be used in coming version.
function FORWARD_callback(**handles**)
//Write your callback for FORWARD here
//Write your callback for FORWARD here
h=openserial(1,"9600,n,8,1");
writeserial(h,"a");
closeserial(h);
endfunction
function REVERSE_callback(**handles**)

```
//Write your callback for REVERSE here
h=openserial(1,"9600,n,8,1");
writeserial(h,"b");
closeserial(h);
endfunction
function LEFT_callback(handles)
//Write your callback for LEFT here
h=openserial(1,"9600,n,8,1");
writeserial(h,"c");
closeserial(h);
endfunction
function RIGHT_callback(handles)
//Write your callback for RIGHT here
h=openserial(1,"9600,n,8,1");
writeserial(h,"d");
closeserial(h);
endfunction
function STOP_callback(handles)
//Write your callback for STOP here
h=openserial(1,"9600,n,8,1");
writeserial(h,"e");
closeserial(h);
endfunction
```

5. Run the sce file, to get the GUI, as shown in Fig. (**13.6**).

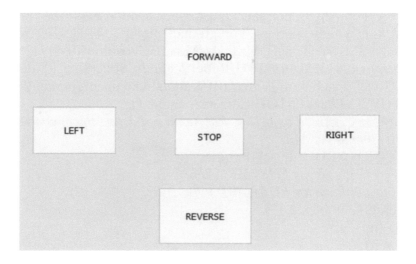

Fig. (13.6). Snapshot of GUI developed in Scilab.

BIBLIOGRAPHY

[1]   R. Singh, A. Gehlot, B. Singh, and S. Choudhury, *Arduino-Based Embedded Systems: Interfacing, Simulation, and LabVIEW GUI* CRC Press: Taylor & Francis, . ISBN 9781138060784.

[2]   R. Singh, A. Gehlot, S. Choudhury, and B. Singh, *Embedded System based on Atmega Microcontroller- Simulation, Interfacing and Projects.*Narosa Publishing House, . ISBN: 978-8-84-7-5720.

[3]   https://www.arduino.cc/en/Main/Software

[4]   https://www.arduino.cc/en/Guide/Windows

SUBJECT INDEX

A

AC Current Sensor 11
AC Voltage Sensor 16
Analog Read with Potentiometer 58
Analog Read with Temprature Sensor 62
Analog Read Write 64
Arduino I/O Package for Scilab 6
Arduino IDE 1
Arduino Mega 3
Arduino Nano 4
Arduino UNO 2
arduino_v3.ino) 48
Arduino 1

B

Blocks of Scilab X 50

C

Capacitive Touch Proximity Sensor 7

D

DC Current Sensor 24
DC Voltage Sensor 21

E

Environment Parameter Monitoring Robot 88
Environment Parameter Monitoring System 82

G

Gas Sensor 84
GSM MODEM 39

I

IR Sensor 83

L

Light Dependent Resistor 70
LM35 84

M

Motion Detection System with Arduino_1.1

P

Package 73
PID Controller for Heater 92
PIR Motion Sensor 74

S

Scilab and GUI without Toolbox 44
Scilab Arduino_1.1 Package (using toolbox_
Scilab GUI 44
Scilab XCOS 50
Serial Communication 29
Servo Motor Control with Arduino_1.1
Package 69
Servo Motor 79

T

Two Axis Solar Tracker 78

W

Wireless Building Automation System 96
Wireless Robot Control 111

www.ingramcontent.com/pod-product-compliance
Lightning Source LLC
LaVergne TN
LVHW071522070326
832902LV00002B/34